D1765022

THE GUARDIAN LIONS
THE SEARCH FOR THE DIVINE PEACH

TIM C. FRANKLIN

THE GUARDIAN LIONS

THE SEARCH FOR THE DIVINE PEACH

TIM C. FRANKLIN

Fully Alive
Sanctuary

First published in the UK by Fully Alive Sanctuary, UK, 2016

Visit the author's website at:
www.theguardianlions.co.uk

Fully Alive Sanctuary
www.fullyalivesanctuary.co.uk

ISBN:
ISBN-978-0-9956512-0-3
Available as digital download and paperback

DEDICATION

The Guardian Lions is dedicated to my children, Eva and Eli. You have been a wonderful source of inspiration, insight, learning and joy.

May you continue to marvel at the wonders life has to offer.

ACKNOWLEDGMENTS

Special thanks goes to my wife Jillie. You have given endless support in my endeavours and passions, for which I am grateful. I would also like to express my sincere appreciation to my friends and partners at Fully Alive – Mark and Barry. You have opened my eyes to the possibilities life has to offer as part of our continued work in helping make the world a safer, happier and healthier place to live. I would also like to pay my respects and express my appreciation to my Sifu, Grandmaster Wong Kiew Kit. Without your generosity and unwavering support for the Shaolin Wahnam family, these stories may never have been realised. You are an inspiration and embodiment of compassion, understanding, wisdom and courage.

CHAPTERS

Earth

Young Guardian Lion. Wise beyond her years, but apparently lacks courage.

Sky

Young Guardian Lion. Full of courage and adventurous, but not very cautious.

Nian

A angry and greedy monster who would appear every Chinese New Year and cause havoc.

Tianlong

A friendly heavenly dragon. Wise, courageous and compassionate.

FOREWORD

From renowned author and Shaolin Grandmaster

Not only children, but also adults and elderly people too love to read stories. However, I do not find many stories that are both interesting to read, and also teach us how to live our lives meaningfully and rewardingly. Stories that satisfy both these qualities are rare indeed. You should not miss a chance to read them. The story here happens to have both these two qualities.

The story here is about two young guardian lions, Earth and Sky, who wish to save Earth's brother, Tao, imprisoned by a warlord who desires to rule the world. The adventures Earth and Sky go through are exciting, tantalizing readers in suspense. To accomplish their mission, the two lions require, among other things, two essential qualities: courage and wisdom. I shall allow the readers to enjoy the excitement of reading the adventures of these two lions in acquiring courage and wisdom, as well as other worthy qualities required to eventually save their brother, Tao.

Besides the fun of reading exciting adventures, the story in the book also teaches readers invaluable lessons to lead their lives meaningfully and rewardingly, like how to overcome fear and anxiety, how to deal with demanding situations calmly and effectively, and how to make the best of the situations we face every day. This book is both interesting to read and educational in the lessons it conveys.

The author, Tim Franklin, is eminently suited for the task. He is a certified instructor of Shaolin Wahnam International, which has more than 60,000 students in over 35 countries worldwide. Besides his own teaching, he teams up with two other certified instructors, Barry Smale and Mark Appleford, to form an organization called Fully Alive that conducts courses to help people overcome illness, enjoy good health, vitality and longevity, and be fully alive every day of their lives.

An invaluable credential that qualifies Tim for this difficult task of writing a book that not only entertains but also teaches readers to deal with life, is that he is happily married with (at present) two lovely children. Tim tells his interesting stories in this book to his two lovely children so that they will benefit from the lessons within to face life joyfully and successfully. This is a book not just to read but also to keep. You will find the adventures both entertaining and educational.

Wong Kiew Kit
Grandmaster
Shaolin Wahnam Institute
www.shaolin.org

INTRODUCTION

Inspired by the Shaolin tradition and the rich history of the Chinese arts, this adventure book takes the reader on a journey of mystical creatures, mild peril and discovery.

'The Guardian Lions' follows the journey of the two main characters, Earth and Sky, as they deal with a variety of challenges we often face growing up. As we have come to understand, dealing with the challenges life has to offer is not always easy, for parent or child.

As a teacher of the Shaolin arts, I was curious about the following questions and ideas: What if we had the tools to deal with life's challenges more skillfully? What would it be like if, instead of feeling locked up or stuck, we could navigate life more freely and easily? Through the arts I practice and teach, that's what I've been finding out.

As a parent myself, I naturally want the best for my children. I want them to grow up being healthy and happy. One way they can do that is to have the right tools and skills to do their best in life.

That's what this book is about. Through the adventures of two young Guardian Lions, Earth and Sky, descendants of the heavenly Guardian Lions to the Emperor - we learn about the struggles we face, such as dealing with fears, feeling alone, finding courage, judgment, handling overwhelming emotions, overcoming violence and aggression, and working with others.

The reason I'm sharing this with you is that I want to pass on some very useful things I have learnt through the study, practice and teaching of the Shaolin arts, things that lead to improved health and happiness - something we can all benefit from.

The Shaolin arts teach how to develop patience, kindness, discipline and respect, as well as how to overcome aggression and avoid violence. Techniques are taught to help relax emotions and channel energy, leading to the child (or adult) feeling calm, more confident, more at ease with themselves and others, as well as with the world around them.

This supports our aims at Fully Alive in doing our part in helping create a world that is healthier, happier and less harmful for the current generation, the children and the grandchildren to live in.

At the Beginning - The Guardian Lions

"When all seems lost, look to the heavens."

As Emperor Gaozu slumped to his knees at the side of his two dying lions, his wife, Empress Lü, stood by and watched motionless, her face fixed like a porcelain doll, devoid of any expression. Only a glint in her eyes and a small crease at the corner of her mouth gave away something more sinister.

The Emperor fell into a great depression. A gift from Persia, these lions had brought great happiness to the Emperor, but now they had gone, and a great cloud descended from

1

the skies, over the lands, and reached into the hearts of the people.

The heavenly beings watched over the Emperor to see what would happen next.

The people prayed to the heavens for the Emperor to find his happiness once more, as he was usually a just, generous and fair ruler. But in his pain he was cruel and unwilling.

Hearing the prayers, two heavenly lions were sent to the Emperor as Guardian Lions to watch over him. The Emperor was delighted and thanked the heavens. These Guardian Lions brought great happiness to the Emperor and once again he spread much joy across the lands.

However, on each Chinese New Year, a monster called Nian would ascend from the sea where he hid and attacked the villages. This was a greedy monster who just loved causing havoc. Most of all, he loved eating children. Being greedy though, he would eat anything in his path. So at this time of year everyone would try to hide away, for fear of being eaten, except for a few farmers who tried to protect their precious crops.

The farmers did their best to drive the monster away, but

it was no use. Unfortunately, Nian was so powerful and greedy that he ate anything in his way, including some of the farmers. Once Nian finished with the farmers, he wandered through the streets, sniffing at doorways, market stalls and carts, looking for something else to eat.

The Emperor had made a promise to the heavens to protect his people from all harm, so he sent his best warriors, the Guardian Lions, to reason with the monster.

When the Guardian Lions arrived at the field they were met by a very fierce, very angry and very greedy monster, Nian. Nian roared at them; he wasn't interested in talking - he just wanted to eat. His roar was so loud that it blew the roofs off the farmers' homes. The Guardian Lions were not afraid and did not move out of the way.

Nian spat out fire at the lions. The Guardian Lions took one step back and moved their paws in circles in front of their bodies, blowing the flames away. Nian was getting angry! He charged at the Guardian Lions, but they simply stepped to the side, out of the way. The monster tripped over and ate dirt.

Nian got up, spitting out dirt. He spun around with his spiky tail at the Guardian Lions. This time they jumped into the air, one landing just in front of him and the other on Nian's back, pinning back his ears to make sure he could hear.

"Why are you fighting with us, monster? Your fight is not with us. You are hungry, but you are also greedy and your greed has made you blind to what you have done. Every year you come to the villages and try to frighten everyone. You eat children and anything in your path. But instead of finding food, you have destroyed the crops the farmers have worked so hard to grow. Now no one has anything to eat, including you. Have you not heard of the mountain of abundance beyond the three seas? There you will find all the food you will ever need. Go now and the heavens will help you find your way."

Nian looked around. Seeing what he had done, he felt ashamed. He knew he was no match for the Guardian Lions, for they possessed great power. It was pointless fighting with them, and they meant him no harm. He was hungry and sorry. The villagers came out of their homes banging pots and pans in celebration and waving red ribbons. Nian could not stand the noise and hated the colour red. With that he bowed to the Guardian Lions and the people, then ran away, never to return. Well, at least not back to the villages.

In honour of the Emperor for sending his two best warriors, the people of the lands held celebrations. Making masks and costumes of the lions, they danced to the beat of drums, hung red lanterns and lit firecrackers to scare away the evil spirits and monsters.

Of course, the Emperor's two Guardian Lions were very skilled - so skilled that they had only needed to use courage and wisdom to help Nian, without causing him unnecessary harm.

The Guardian Lions fought many battles for the Emperor and helped protect the people from unhelpful spirits, creatures and monsters. The more they fought, the more would come, until there were too many for the Guardian Lions to fight alone. The Guardian Lions decided it was time to talk with the Emperor. While the Guardian Lions were more powerful in kung fu abilities than the Emperor, they also knew their place and considered themselves the Emperor's servants sent from the heavens to protect and serve. Upon arriving at his court, they bowed and waited permission to speak.

"What news do you bring me?" the Emperor asked.

"It is not good news, Your Imperial Majesty," said one of

the lions. "We have fought with and won over the hearts and minds of a thousand monsters and creatures. Yet still, more come." "I see," the Emperor said. "This is not good. I had hoped that by now the monsters and creatures would know it was useless trying to fight against us."

"We had wished this too, Your Imperial Majesty. All we have fought with have retreated peacefully. Yet, there are whisperings... whisperings for Your Imperial Majesty's throne."

The Emperor smashed his fists down on the table. "This is ridiculous; who would dare challenge me with you two at my side?"

"Agreed, Your Imperial Majesty. We believe the reason for the vast numbers of monsters and creatures attacking the villages is to keep us away from Your Imperial Majesty's side. To overwhelm us with numbers, and to prove Your Imperial Majesty unfit to rule."

The Emperor stroked his long beard to consider what the Guardian Lions had told him.

"This is a conundrum. What is your solution?" asked the Emperor.

"We have been Your Imperial Majesty's loyal guards for many years. It is our duty and honour to serve at Your Imperial Majesty's side. Yet we alone cannot cover enough ground to keep Your Imperial Majesty and the people safe. We should ask the heavens to send more lions to protect the people."

"What if the lions fell into the hands of our enemies and are turned against your Emperor or the people we protect?"

"Your Imperial Majesty, the lions won't be heavenly lions like us. They will be descendants of the heavenly lions. Each will possess enough skills to protect the lands, but not have our power. When we die we will pass our power onto another keeper. Your Imperial Majesty will be safe all the time we are at Your Imperial Majesty's side."

Agreeing with this proposal, the Emperor handed the Guardian Lions the royal seal to show the heavens to proceed with the plan. From then on, all the villages and lands had real heavenly lions to protect and bring joy, not just ones they'd made for the celebrations from masks and costumes.

The Emperor Gaozu of Han enjoyed a protected reign from his Guardian Lions for a number of years. But then it was time for him to die and pass on his legacy to his son, Liu Ying, who would become Emperor Hui.

After the death of his younger half-brother Ruyi, Emperor Hui became concerned for his own safety. In fear of his successors using the Guardian Lions for wrongdoing, he had them turned to stone. But not before their spirit and power were hidden in waiting, for the descendants of the Guardian Lions to be ready to receive and harness the power.

For nearly 2000 years, the power of the Guardian Lions was passed down from Guardian to Guardian, to protect the people of the lands and keep the peace. Now a fortuneteller has given knowledge of the next passing of power to a warlord – a warlord who wants to steal this power and become supreme ruler under the heavens.

Tao and The Tomb

"Courage is not the absence of fear, but the mastery of it." - Victor Hugo

Rubbing the torn piece of red cloth between her paws, Earth sniffed it, opened her 'Book of Things' and carefully placed it inside. Regretting having wished he never existed, Earth desperately hoped the cloth would lead to the whereabouts of her missing brother.

"How could you do this to me, Tao?" Earth said, with tears rolling down the fur on her cheek. It was time to face her parents.

"Earth, your brother still hasn't returned. We're worried

about him and it's getting dark. Do you have any idea where he could have gone? Does he have a secret hideout in the hills? We know you both go to the hills to play. You're always gone for hours," said Earth's mother.

"It's not my fault, Ma."

"I'm not saying it is, Earth. But last time I saw him was just after you two had a big fight, and he was heading to the hills. I was just hoping you might have a clue."

"What do you mean, a clue? Why would I have a clue? It's his fault anyway. It's his fault he ran off," Earth said.

"What was it you were fighting about anyway?"

"Nothing," Earth said.

"It can't have been nothing, otherwise he wouldn't have run off so upset."

"It was nothing, I told you," Earth said.

"I'm not cross with you, Earth, just worried for Tao. If you know anything, anything at all, I would really like to know. Please."

"You promise that if I tell you what we were fighting about, you won't be cross with me."

"I promise," said her mother.

Earth waited silently for a few moments, staring at her mother's face for a sign that she might be deceiving her. Her mother looked back with an honesty that pulled at Earth's heart.

"Tao found something in the hills. He was going back for it. I told him to leave it alone but he wouldn't listen."

Earth's mother tilted her head to one side and narrowed her large eyes.

"You don't believe me. You don't believe what I'm telling you. It's true. I told him it was bad. But he went anyway," Earth said.

"Earth, calm down. I'm just surprised, that's all. You're normally the first one to discover things, to collect things. What is it that you didn't want your brother to have?"

Earth looked down at the floor, unable to look her mother in the face.

"Earth, what is it you are not telling me? What are you afraid of? I told you, I will not be cross. I just want to help."

"He found a tomb," Earth said, still looking at the ground. Her mother's eyes widened.

"What do you mean, he found a tomb?"

"I mean a tomb Ma, a tomb," Earth said.

"Whose tomb?"

"I don't know. But something was wrong about it. I could feel it."

"So why didn't Tao listen to you?"

"I tried Ma, I really did. But he kept saying it was something he needed to do. Like it was his destiny."

"Can you show me where the tomb is, Earth?"

"Yes, I drew a map of it in my Book of Things." Earth's mother looked pleased at this.

"Ok, we have to go now."

"But you said it's getting dark, Ma."

"I know, so we better move quick," said her mother.

Earth had the feeling that her mother was holding something back.

"What are you not telling me, Ma?"

"There's no time to explain now, Earth. Hopefully we are not too late."

"Too late for what?" Earth said.

"I'll have to explain later. Right now we need to go."

"What about Pa?"

"There's no time," her mother said, before running off at speed.

Earth hadn't seen her mother move this fast in years and found it hard to keep up.

"Take the path on the right," Earth called out.

Her mother was already halfway up the hill, heading

towards the tomb when Earth caught sight of a silhouette looking down from the top of the hill. She instantly knew it wasn't her brother. This figure stood tall on two legs, with a cloak flapping in the wind. Pushing down on her back legs, Earth desperately tried to catch up with her mother. When she looked up again, the figure had gone. Her mother had already reached the top of the hill and was heading directly for the tomb.

When Earth caught up, her mother was standing motionless at the entrance of the tomb.

"We're too late, Earth. It's already happened."

"What's happened, Ma? I don't understand."

"We tried to hide this from you both, hoping that somehow the prophecy would be wrong. We should have seen this coming. Your father warned me."

"Warned you against what, Ma? Where's Tao? Why aren't you going inside to look for him?"

"It's no use, Earth. I cannot enter the tomb."

"Then I'll go in," Earth said.

14

"It won't work Earth, only Tao can enter the tomb."

"So he could still be in there then?"

"Unfortunately not, Earth. The figure you saw on the hill was a lookout. Tao is already gone."

"So we go back home and get Pa, he'll help find Tao."

Earth's mother nodded in agreement. "I'll let your father explain this one."

When they returned home, Earth's father was waiting at the door.

"It's happened," said Earth's mother.

Her father let out a long sigh. "You'd better sit down Earth, I have something to tell you."

Earth sat down on a log, fearing the worst.

"Earth, there's no easy way to tell you this. Your brother has been taken," her father said.

Earth was actually a little relieved, in an odd way. At least he was alive. "Who's taken him, Pa? Why would someone take Tao?"

"Bad people, Earth. Very bad people."

"What do they want with him? Why Tao, Pa?"

"Because of who he is, Earth," said her father.

"What do you mean? He's just my brother."

"That he is Earth, but he is also a chosen descendant of the Heavenly Lions, and when the planets align his power will be revealed. The bad people want that power."

"But we are all descendants of the Heavenly Lions Pa, aren't we?"

"We are, Earth. But Tao is different; he has been chosen by the Guardian Lions. These lions had very special powers, powers that Tao will soon receive."

"That's not fair, why haven't I got these powers, or you or Ma? Why Tao?"

"It is not for me to question the work of the heavens, Earth. They chose Tao for this path; you will have your own path to follow. To be honest, your Ma and I were hoping the prophecy would not be true. We knew this wouldn't be easy for any of us. All we want for both of you is to be happy and safe. That's all."

Earth turned her back. "Well, it's still not fair."

"Tomorrow we will send out a search party for your brother. We have very good trackers in this village," her father said. "Now, try and get some sleep."

Earth went inside to her room and lay down on her bed.

"My own brother, a chosen one," she scoffed.

Hold on, that means I could also be a chosen one. Perhaps my parents just don't want to tell me yet, she thought to herself. And that means I should be the one to find him. I'll wait until my parents go to sleep, then sneak out in search of him.

Earth thought her plan was perfect. Except she had no idea how to find him. All she had was a piece of cloth and the location of a tomb. Perhaps she could consult her Book of Things. It was full of amazing facts and interesting things she had discovered. The 'Book of Things', with the cover made from a dragon scale, was unlike her other books. It contained all that she knew, and things that she didn't.

Somehow, things just appeared in there when she needed them most. Earth opened the book at a random page, hoping the location of her brother would present itself. The page was blank. She turned to another page. It was a silly poem about nothing. In anger she threw the book to the ground.

Confused in her feelings, Earth stared at the ceiling. There was no doubt that Earth was wise beyond her years. She knew things a lion of her age wouldn't normally know. But right now, all the books she had read, the nature she had studied, and her knowledge of monsters and creatures, all felt worthless. She felt afraid.

Earth looked at her book on the floor. What was the point? she thought. Even if it did have a map to my brother, I can't go alone. But no matter how much she tried to ignore her feelings of fear, deep down she knew that somehow she needed to summon the courage to go. She should be the one to find him. Now all she needed was to know where to start looking. She looked at the piece of torn red cloth, put her book in her satchel and waited quietly for her parents to fall asleep.

Everything was quiet, all except for the sound of her father's snore. She walked quietly to her bedroom door and opened it slowly. It creaked. Her father's snore changed from its usual long rhythm to a sudden sucking in of air, like a saw through a log.

"Wha-what is that?" he murmured in his sleep. Earth paused for a moment and waited for his usual snore to return, then crept quietly past her parents' bedroom. The front door was bolted and locked from the inside. Earth reached up to the usual hanging place for a key; it wasn't there.

"Are you looking for these?" Earth turned around and came face to face with her father, hanging the keys out in front of him.

"I just needed to get some air," Earth said, without thinking. Her father stared back with a look of disbelief.

"Earth, I took the keys because I knew you would try to find your brother alone. It's what I would have done. But I can't let you go. You don't know who you are dealing with," her father said.

"If I don't go, Tao might die. And it'll be my..." Earth stopped what she was saying.

"It will be what, Earth? Your fault?" her father said. "How could this be your fault?"

"I should have stopped him. You don't understand. I shouldn't have said the things I did."

"Try me, Earth. I am willing to listen," Earth's father said.

"I don't want to talk; I just want to find him. Why are you holding me back?" Earth replied.

"I'm not holding you back, Earth. I'm trying to protect you."

"Protect me? Protect me... and let your, your son die?" said Earth.

"We're not going to let Tao die, Earth. We'll find him," said her father.

"Then let me find him. Let me go," said Earth. Earth's father knew it would not be easy to convince Earth to stay. He also knew he wouldn't be able to hold her captive either.

"Ok, Earth," her father said. But before he could finish his sentence, Earth interrupted.

"So I can go then?" Earth said, making her way to the door.

"What I was going to say, Earth, is you can accompany the trackers. They leave at sunrise. You can go with them. Now get some sleep and we'll see you off in the morning."

Earth tried to hide her disappointment. Of course she was pleased her father was letting her go, but she wanted to go alone. She was used to doing things her way and knew the trackers would be under strict instructions to keep a close eye on her.

"Earth," her father said.

Earth thought it best to hide her feelings so thanked her father and went back to her bedroom. She lay back on her bed and tried to come up with a plan of escape. This was meant to be her quest, not the trackers'.

In a Hole

"The path to this is simple to find, yet, not so easy to follow." - The wise old man on the hill

S ky called out from the hole where moments before he had been lying in a crumpled heap. "Is anyone there?"

Brushing the dirt off his matted fur with his oversized lion paws, he waited for an answer. He called out again. There was no reply. Satisfied that no one had seen him fall into the hole, he released his puffed up chest and sat down, feeling deflated and alone.

"Argh, why can't I jump this simple hole?" But there was

no time for self-pity. The sound of crunching ground from above alerted Sky to something approaching. He stood up and readied himself. Shadows of animals leapt over the hole, darting in all directions. A lion's face appeared over the edge of the hole, followed by another, then another. A large, rotund face squeezed its way to the front.

"Oh, it's you again," the young, but rather overweight lion said. "What's the matter, Sky? Fell down another hole, did you!"

The lion's cronies laughed. Sky shrunk deeper into the already deep hole.

"You'll never be able to jump it, you're too small. Here, let me help you," the lion said, stretching out his paw down towards Sky.

Sky hesitated, having fallen for his dirty tricks before. Perhaps this time was different though. Maybe he actually felt sorry for Sky, who was smaller than the other lions of his age. Sky reached up and took his paw. The lion smiled kindly and started to pull Sky up. But just as he reached the top, the smile turned to a grin, and he let Sky go. Sky fell hard on his back

"Oh, sorry Sky, I lost my grip."

The lion's cronies snorted in laughter as they walked away, leaving Sky down in the hole. Sky slumped against the walls of the hole, tears running down the fur on his face.

A large muscular paw reached over the edge, followed by an even larger head with a single curved horn, big green eyes and a huge grinning mouth.

"Come on son. Here, take my paw," Sky's father said. Sky looked at the ground, feeling a little ashamed, and grabbed his father's paw.

"Thanks Pa. I hate those goons, I really do. They're always bullying and playing tricks on me."

"Come on son. You really don't need to worry about them. You've got nothing to prove to them or me. You're fine the way you are. Right now though you need to come home and help us prepare for the New Year celebrations."

Sky was wishing though he had more wisdom and ability, instead of just being fearless. That way he would be able to show those bullies he wasn't someone to mess with. And he knew just the person to help him - the wise old man on the rock. His father was busy climbing a pole, hanging a lantern. Sky was sure he wouldn't miss him for a few minutes if he crept off.

When he arrived, the wise old man was sitting quietly on the rock looking out over the village below, with his eyes closed. "Excuse me," Sky said to the wise old man, "what is the best way for me to jump further?"

He wasn't sure if the wise old man had heard, because he did not move or open his eyes. After a short pause, he spoke.

"It is not how you jump, but what comes before you jump." The wise old man fell silent.

Sky did not understand the riddle, but he didn't care too much; he was feeling glad the wise old man had listened and given him a proper answer. Well, kind of.

When he arrived back in the village his father was waiting, looking stern.

"I thought you agreed to help, Sky. It's not ok for you to keep running off like this. You need to take responsibility, Sky. Now, go and practice your kung fu. No slacking this time. If you want to become great, you have to practice."

Sky went to the courtyard at the front of his house and jumped onto the wooden poles that stood several feet high. Moving from pole to pole, he went through his kung fu stances until his legs could take no more. He must have lost track of time and practiced for hours, as it was now dark.

That night, lying in bed, Sky kept playing the riddle over in his head.

'It is not how you jump, but what comes before you jump'.

He wondered what the riddle could mean. *If only I understood what he meant, I would be able to jump further.* With that he fell into a deep sleep.

Sky was dreaming about running and leaping and jumping when he stopped by a very large hole. The hole was so big that he couldn't even see the other side. Through the clouds covering the middle of the hole, a dragon appeared. The dragon flew through the clouds, diving, disappearing and then reappearing as it drew closer to Sky.

The dragon flew right up to Sky, hovering in the air. "Hello,

Sky. You seem troubled; is there something I can help you with?"

The dragon was Tianlong, a very old and wise heavenly dragon.

"I wish I could jump this hole, but I can't run fast enough or jump high enough. The wise old man told me it is not how I jump, but what comes before I jump. But I don't understand," Sky replied.

"You are a very brave warrior Sky, you have much courage, that is for sure. But without wisdom, courage alone can lead to foolish decisions. You are not a fool, but you need to find wisdom to find your answer," explained Tianlong.

"How do I find wisdom, Tianlong?" Sky asked eagerly.

"You will find wisdom with the divine peach, this is where you must go to find what you are looking for." With that, Tianlong slipped away into the clouds.

When Sky woke the next morning, he really felt like his dream had been real. He asked his mum if she had heard of the divine peach. She had heard stories about the divine peach when she was small, but she didn't believe they were true, so couldn't tell Sky where it was. Sky asked his father if he had heard of the divine peach. He had, but he warned Sky that the journey was too dangerous for a young lion like him, and that he should stay home and practice his kung fu.

Sky decided to ask the wise old man who lived on the rock. Sure enough, the wise old man was sitting on the rock, looking over the village with his eyes closed.

"Excuse me wise old man," Sky asked politely. "Can you tell me how to find the divine peach tree?"

The wise old man cleared his throat. "Mmm, let me see. The divine peach tree you seek, the path to this is simple to find, yet not so easy to follow. Go to the river, where you'll find your first step. From there you will find nature's way. Many have missed its path as they rush ahead. All you need to do is listen, with more than your ears, and see, with more than your eyes."

Sky thanked the wise old man and left. He was beginning to wonder though quite how wise the old man was, because every time he spoke it was in riddles.

Leaping off the rock, Sky made his way down to the village

to tell his parents he needed to go on an adventure. They tried to persuade him not to go, but could see in his eyes that this was something he needed to do.

"Take this with you Sky, it will protect you." His father handed him a pendant that had been handed down through the generations. It was a pearl, held by a clasp around the top in a shape of a dragon's foot, made from gold and attached to a leather string.

Sky thanked his father, hugged his mother, who had tears in her eyes, and turned towards the direction of the river. He was excited about his adventure, and now that he had the pendant he felt invincible.

When he arrived at the river, he searched around for what might be his first step. There was a large rock just near the river edge. He leapt on top to see if this could be 'the first step'. This place didn't feel right. Sky could see across the river, but he knew it was too wide to jump.

Sky jumped off the rock and looked further up the river. It was wider than he remembered, and at this time of the year was flowing really fast. He would have to find a safe place to cross if he wanted to avoid falling in. He walked a little further upstream to find the 'first step'. As hard as he looked, Sky could not see any steps. The old man must have been fooling him. He would go back to the old man and tell him just what he thought of his silly riddles. Turning around to go back, he heard a voice.

"It is not how you jump, but what comes before you jump. Listen with more than your ears, see with more than your eyes."

"Another riddle," he shouted. "That's no help!"

Then he heard the voice again. "Go to the river, where you'll find your first step. From there you will find nature's way."

"That's no help either," Sky said. "I don't get the riddles, I'm trying to find a step or path or nature's way, but all I see in front of me is a river."

With that, Sky sat down for a rest. After a while, he had a thought. *Perhaps the old man didn't mean a real path or step, perhaps he meant I had to find my own way. But what did he mean by 'nature's way'? Or 'what comes before the jump'? Or 'listen with more than my ears and see with more than my eyes'?*

Sky got up to venture further up the river. He was in luck! There was a fallen tree lying across the river. He could use this as a bridge. Sky was great at climbing, so this should be easy.

Excited, Sky bounded up towards the fallen tree and leapt onto the trunk. It creaked. *Not to worry*, he thought, *I'll soon be across.*

Halfway across, the trunk split off into branches. The branch to the left looked stronger, so he continued walking across. There was a creak, then a crack. Sky started to hurry his pace. Then another big crack behind him. The branch was about to snap and he was still several feet from the other side.

CRACK!!!!

The branched snapped. Without thinking, Sky took one big leap. His front paws reached the bottom edge of the riverbank. The bank was soggy from the heavy rainfalls and he could feel his grip slipping. With no time to think, he quickly brought his back legs close to his front legs, and with all his might he jumped to the top of the bank.

Looking back he could see the broken branch floating

down the river.

"That was close; maybe next time I'll test the branch before I step on it."

Where should I go now? Sky pondered. *Now that I have crossed the river, I'm supposed to find nature's way!*

Sky looked around for something obvious to show the way, but all he could see around him was grass and trees in the distance. An eagle squawked above Sky as it circled around the wispy white clouds. The sound got louder as it swooped past and flew off into the distance. Within a minute, the eagle was back again, squawking and swooping. Before long the sound of the bird began to irritate Sky.

"Will you just go away?" he said to the eagle. "Can't you see I'm trying to think here!" The eagle just kept swooping and squawking.

It's no use, he thought. *I'll never be able to find nature's way with all this noise.* Sensing Sky's frustration, the eagle landed on a small patch of flattened grass where Sky had been pacing around. Sky looked at the eagle and the eagle looked back. Sky was sure the eagle let out a sigh and shook its head as if in disbelief.

"What?" Sky said, looking at the eagle.

The eagle turned its head towards the distant trees, pointing with its beak. Sky shrugged his shoulders, as if to show he did not understand. So the eagle pointed its beak again at the trees in the distance and took flight back into the clouds.

"Oh," Sky said. "I get it; you want me to follow you to the trees. You are nature's way." With that, the eagle turned its head approvingly towards Sky, nodded and took flight.

As Sky ran through the long grass towards the forest, he had a feeling of excitement rush through his body, filling him with energy as he went. For fleeting moments, it felt like his paws were not even touching the ground as he galloped towards the forest. As Sky neared the edge of the forest, he noticed the Eagle was no longer there. All he could see was a dark, dark, deep forest.

Sky was not afraid; he was on a quest. He puffed up his chest, just like he did before he jumped a big hole, and strode boldly into the forest. Once in the forest, Sky realised that there was no obvious path to lead the way. Unsure which way to go, he continued on, deeper into the forest. The deeper he got, the closer together the trees got, making it difficult to get through. Was he lost? Was he going to have to give up and turn around, he wondered? There was no time to answer this as his attention darted towards the crunching sound of branches breaking. He was not alone.

"Who's there…?" Sky called out.

There was no reply.

"Show yourself, I won't hurt you," Sky said.

There was no reply.

Probably just a bear or something, Sky thought, unfazed by the noise.

Looking for a better route, he doubled back on himself. Before long, he found a clearing with a large tree. *This would be a good place for a camp*, he thought.

Gathering some branches, Sky started to put together a dome-shaped shelter. Settling down inside the dome, he lay back and looked up to the stars that were beginning their nightly duty.

This is great, he thought, feeling very pleased with himself.

I love making things. *I'll stop here for the night and set off tomorrow to find the divine peach.*

Sky woke up early to practice his kung fu exercises. He enjoyed his daily practice; it gave him lots of energy and the feeling of strength and courage. His forms were beautiful to watch, full of movement, leaping and excitement. Once he had finished his practice, his thoughts turned to where he should go next. "I know, I'll go where the wind blows me," he said aloud. "That way I'll be following nature's way."

Sky waited for some wind, yet the air was still. "Mmm, then I'll listen for something to give me a sign."

He turned his head from one side to the other, stretching his ears for the right sound to guide him. This didn't help either, as all he could hear was the sound of birds in each direction.

"Right... I'll walk around until I see something interesting."

Sky walked about for some time. There were plenty of interesting things to see in the forest, but he was not sure which one he should pick. Frustrated, he grabbed two sticks from the ground and started drumming the trees as he walked by.

A large tree stump caught his attention, so he headed towards it, eager to test it out. It was unlike the neighbouring trees. This tree stump must have been thousands of years old. Yet it had been cut with precision. Sky tapped the side of it. It was solid and gave out a metallic sound. *That's odd*, he thought. He struck the top a few times in succession. The trunk gave out a resounding boom, like it was hollow. *Odd indeed. It's like my lion drum,* Sky thought.

As well as practicing kung fu, Sky was also learning the Lion Dance. The Lion Dance consisted of drumming, cymbals, a gong and lots of moving, leaping and climbing – all the things that Sky just loved to do. When Sky wasn't leaping or climbing, he was either practicing his kung fu or his Lion Dance. Of course he was supposed to help his parents too, but to Sky that was just boring.

The feeling of freedom Sky got from his practice encouraged him to practice every day. When he was in full flow, it was like nothing could stop him – no boundaries, no limits. It was a wonderful feeling.

Sometimes, when Sky was feeling frustrated or angry, he would go off and practice his kung fu or play the drums of the Lion Dance as a way to calm down.

Practicing the repetitive movements of the kung fu sets, Sky felt free. And the rhythmic sound of the drum had a meditative effect on Sky, and on those around him. The drum was large, like a short barrel, like this tree trunk, and as you might imagine the sound of the drum could travel quite far.

Well, whilst Sky was drumming away on the tree stump to let go of his frustration, the beats of the drum travelled through the forest.

Breaking his usual rhythm of 'da la da dum, da la da dum, da la da dumdumdumdumdum', Sky started to play freely. It was like the sound was coming from his heart, instead of his head... It was effortless and he felt happy! Da dadumdum, da dadumdum, da dum, da dum, da dadumdum...

He was so lost in the playing that he didn't notice the creatures from the forest gathering around the edges of the clearing. Sky looked up to notice a hundred eyes looking back at him.

Leap of Faith

"Once you have made a decision to do something, do it wholeheartedly."

Exhausted from her efforts of attempted escape, Earth laid back on her bed. As her mind drifted, she found herself at the side of a small river. The river was just too wide for her to leap across, and as she stood there wondering how she would get across, a large branch came floating towards her. She uncharacteristically leapt onto the branch and onto the bank on the other side of the river.

From there she was being pulled towards a dark, dark forest. This was a dark and dangerous forest, not the sort of place you would want to venture into alone, especially if you were afraid of the unknown. But Earth knew she must venture inside if she was going to have any hope of finding her brother. It wouldn't be long until it was dark. Earth had to get moving.

Quickening her pace, Earth ran into the forest – deeper and deeper she went. Before long though she came across the same trees and stumps she had already passed. *How could this be?* she thought – she had been going in a straight line. The trouble was that rarely does one travel in a straight path, especially when in a dark, dark forest.

Earth set off again, snapping a small branch every twenty paces she took. That way she would be sure to find her way. It was now getting dark and cold. If she was going to make it through the night, she would have to find shelter.

In the distance, Earth saw a wisp of smoke rising through the trees. A small hut hid in a hollow near a clump of trees. It looked inviting, with a small glow of yellow light beaming just enough through the small window to show the way. She knocked on the old wooden door. A little old lady opened it, greeting Earth with a welcome grin, as if she was expected.

Earth entered the tiny hut and looked around the room. There was a fire glowing warmly in the corner, with a pot of the delicious smelling food bubbling away. She sat down on a wooden stool; her head felt a little woozy. Tired, she closed her eyes.

Earth was back in the thick of the forest. She sat down on a stump and began to cry. She was frightened and alone, unsure of what had just happened. The trees around her began to give a gentle whisper. There was a faint rhythmic sound.

Da dadumdum, da dadumdum, da dum, da dum, da dadumdum... The sound repeated.

What was that sound?

Getting up from the stump, Earth walked around to find the source of the sound. The sound continued. There, between the thick of the trees, she could just make out the outline of a creature. But oddly, the sound continued in the opposite direction. The creature seemed to be attracted to the sound, moving towards it cautiously through the trees, as if to stay out of sight.

A beam of light shone through the canopy of trees, and for

a split moment Earth was sure she saw two horns gleaming in the sun's rays. Was this Chi' Lin, the mystical unicorn?

At this she woke up from her dream. It was sunrise already and time to leave with the trackers. Earth knew what she had to do. Somehow she would escape the trackers and head for the dark, dark forest across the stream. Whatever lay in store for her now was already written; she had seen it in her dream. This was not the first time she had seen things before they happened.

As they reached a bend in the river, Earth signaled to the trackers that she needed to ease herself, and needed a little privacy.

"Don't wait for me," Earth called out. "I'll catch up with you."

Earth headed off towards the river and crouched down next to a rock, out of sight. The unsuspecting trackers continued along the path.

Earth waited a little longer, until she was sure the trackers wouldn't see her.

Standing at the river's edge, she paused.

"What am I doing? I can't do this." Earth got a sick feeling, deep in the pit of her stomach. Her heart began to race; a feeling of panic rose up from within.

"There's no way I'm prepared for this; I don't even know what I'm heading into. I have to do this! My brother needs me." With her book in her paw, she set off to the river. Once at the river she stopped again. Her paws were sweaty, and the feeling of dread and fear was starting to overwhelm her.

Earth stood there for some time, one moment looking in the direction of the trackers, the next with a look of turning around and going home, then boldly walking up to the edge of the river, readying herself to cross.

Earth was confused and admittedly scared. She had to find her courage.

Earth pictured her brother helpless in chains. "I have to do this for my brother," she said, determined to save him.

Looking at the river, she wondered how she was going to get across. It was just too wide to jump and flowing too fast to wade across. If she fell in, she would get swept away for sure. Falling in would be disastrous. Not only was Earth not yet a confident swimmer, but she also had a fear of water. Her heart fluttered, missing a beat. Then she remembered her dream.

That's ok, I'll just wait for the log to float down and I'll jump on that, she thought, feeling quite confident. Then she was filled will dread again from the fear of falling in. What was she to do? She couldn't turn back now. She had to do it. But where was the log?

Just around the bend of the river she could see a log coming towards her, just like in her dream. *This is it, she thought. This is my chance and I have to do it!*

As the log approached, her legs shook. Twenty feet... ten feet... five feet... and she leapt!

As Earth landed on the log, one end tipped down into the water, almost throwing her off. Quickly shifting her weight, she lifted her front paws into the air and stood on one leg. The log balanced out. From here she sprung effortlessly onto the upper side of the bank. A feeling of pride and accomplishment washed over her body. If it hadn't been for her vision, perhaps she would never have summoned the courage to take the leap of faith.

Composing herself, Earth made her way towards the dark, dark forest. At the edge of the forest she stopped. If she rushed ahead she would surely get lost. Then she remembered part of her vision. Every twenty paces or so, she snapped a small branch. But despite her best efforts, she still hadn't found a main path and she was feeling lost. This angered her. Except for her fears, Earth was used to being in control and getting things right.

She sat down and opened her 'Book of Things', with a cover made from the scale of a dragon. *Perhaps there is something in here that can help me*, she thought hopefully. Many of the pages in the book had been written by Earth: things she had discovered herself, drawings she had made, descriptions of potions and spells, plants that could heal, songs that could bring things to life. Other pages seemed to just appear from nowhere and she had no idea how they got there.

As she flipped through the pages, Earth paused on a page with a map. The map had a river to the right hand side of the page, a forest in the middle and a mountain range on the left. This was one of those pages that just appeared. Wherever it had come from, she was grateful, for it was a map of where she was. Earth recognised on the map the bend in the river where she had crossed. On the map of the forest was a rock in the shape of a turtle. Not far from the rock she could see a path in the forest. All she needed to do was find that rock.

Curious Nature

"A curious nature is like a door to another world."

Earth looked around her for signs of the rock in her book. If she found the rock she would find her way. In each direction, all she could see was the trees of the dark, dark forest. She felt truly lost and scared, but she was not about to give up. She looked around for a tall tree, something she could get a better view from. Close by, she spotted a tree with a large trunk and branches spread like a staircase. Leaping onto the lowest branch, she started to climb.

Before long she had already climbed up twenty feet. Stopping for a moment's breath, Earth looked down. Her legs trembled as the thought of falling entered her mind. Earth was afraid of heights; even so, she knew there was no choice other than to climb. So she climbed and climbed until she could climb no further. From the top of the tree she could see over the whole forest. In the distance she could see a large rock in the shape of a turtle. This was the rock on her map!

Excited, Earth started to climb down, and then stopped. Something from the corner of her eye caught her attention. It was a thin wisp of smoke rising through the canopy of the treetops between her and the rock. She got a sinking feeling in the pit of her stomach, as if knowing something bad was going to happen. She climbed down and cautiously made her way to where the wisp of smoke was coming from. The smoke was coming from a small hut hidden deep in a hollow in the woods.

The old rundown shack had seen better days. The roof, made of bark, had holes in it, caused by years of neglect or by the impact of an object falling from the sky. The windows flapped open and shut, banging against the logged wooden exterior. The low oval-shaped door was open. Twigs lay strewn across the verandah, as if the place was abandoned. Earth crouched, nervously looking at the hut. *Who could live here?* she thought.

She looked around, noticing the darkness of the evening approaching. Before long it would be nighttime. The thought of being alone in the dark worried her. Dubiously, she made her way towards the hut. As she got closer, a smell of something delicious cooking wafted towards her. Earth's stomach gave an involuntary gurgling rumble. Looking through the small opening of the window, Earth could make out the shape of an old lady bent over a pot of bubbling broth. Continuing to stir, without moving her body, the old lady cranked her neck around to look at Earth. Earth jumped back in fright.

"Don't be afraid, come in, come in, the door's open," the old lady said in a soft, inviting voice.

Earth made her way to the front door, not sure whether or not to come in.

"It will soon be dark," the old lady smiled, "and there are far worse things than me out there you need to fear."

Earth stepped into the hut, looking around the room as she moved closer to the old lady. The walls were covered with pots and trinkets and strange objects Earth had not seen before. In the corner of room was a small pot, with a disgusting, decaying, smelly black substance in it that moved and wriggled on its own. Earth quickly looked away back towards the old lady.

"Please sit... sit," the old lady invited, pointing towards a chair carved from a log. Earth sat down as requested.

"You must be hungry?" the old lady asked while passing a bowl of soup under Earth's nose. As her taste buds came alive, there was no denying that Earth was hungry. She accepted the food graciously.

Earth finished up her meal, stood up and handed back the bowl. "You are very kind, but I really must be off now."

"Nonsense, you can't go.... I mean it's dangerous out there at nighttime. Things in the forest that will eat you before you can jump. Better stay here tonight and you can go in the morning. Where is it you are going?" the old lady asked, changing the subject.

"I'm not exactly sure," Earth said, for the first time really realising that actually, she didn't know. "I just know that I need to find my brother - he's been taken." Earth wasn't sure why she shared this piece of information with the old lady.

"Oh, that sounds dreadful. I wish there was something I could do to help, but I am old and frail, and can barely manage to collect my own wood for the fire. Be a good little lion, would you, and grab the logs outside the front door and bring them in. It's going to be a cold night tonight."

Earth couldn't remember seeing logs outside the front, just twigs. Sure enough though, there was a pile of logs outside, just as the old lady had said. She brought in enough for the night and placed them carefully on the floor next to the fire pit with the pot above.

As Earth sat down again, the old lady handed her some tea, before placing some more logs on the fire. The tea had an unusual flavour. Not unpleasant in any way, just unusual. Finishing the tea, Earth felt tired. It must have been the journey, she thought. With her eyes heavy, she drifted off into a deep sleep. Images swirled around her head. She was surrounded by trees, running through the forest, but getting nowhere. Something was pulling her back. She made a break for it, falling into a pool of water. The water dragged her down, deeper and deeper. Then she was in a cave; it was dark and damp, and there was a rank smell of the breath of a monster over her shoulder. She tried to run but everything was in slow motion. No matter how hard she tried to move away from the smell and breath, it just followed her. Then everything went pitch black. It was so dark that she couldn't even see her paws in front of her eyes. Trying to move or run away was useless, so she sat down and waited.

The sound of pans clattering woke Earth from her deep sleep. "Ah, good morning," a voice said from across the room. "You're awake. Did you sleep well?"

Earth was not sure where she was; everything was a blur. She felt dazed, her limbs heavy and tired.

"You had quite a nightmare last night," the old lady said knowingly. "Would you like some tea, something to eat perhaps?" the old lady enquired sweetly. Earth opened her mouth to answer, but no words came out, just a look of confusion on her face.

"You don't look too well, perhaps you should rest some more. The journey here must have really taken a toll on you." the old lady said with a concerned look on her face.

Earth knew she had to get out of there. She had to save her brother. However, with not enough energy to stand, she couldn't go anywhere. Was her dream coming true? Was the old lady really a monster? Had she been poisoned? All these questions were whizzing around Earth's head, making her more and more dizzy. She felt useless.

The old lady, sensing Earth's confusion, seized the opportunity to offer her more tea. "Drink it. It will make you feel better."

Earth sipped the tea from the china cup, as the old lady continued to tip it towards her mouth, until it was finished.

Within a few minutes Earth was feeling much better. She was convinced the old lady had tried to poison her with the tea, still, here she was having drunk the tea and feeling better. Perhaps she was wrong about the old lady. Getting back on her feet and walking around the room, Earth noticed the black sticky, smelly substance in a pot. Was it possible that she was just tired, as the old lady had said, and in her dream she could smell the stench of the black substance? Perhaps!

"I really need to get going now. You've been very kind letting me stay here, but I must go." Earth thanked the old lady.

"Of course, of course you must," the old lady said, nodding. "Just before you go though, could you help me with something? I just can't do it alone and I don't know when I'll see anyone again this way. It's been years since I've had company." Her voice trailed off as she looked down at the floor.

Earth felt a tug in her heart. How could she just go when the old lady had been so kind? Looking up, the old lady continued her request. "At the top of the tree with the darkest of bark is a bug I need for my concoction. You know, the one with the foul smell." She tilted her head towards Earth. "All you need to do is get the bug and bring it to me. That's it, then you are free to continue your quest."

Earth was free to go now, if she wanted to. However, she was curious about what was so special about this bug and why the lady needed it for her concoction. She was also curious to know what the concoction was for.

"I must warn you, though." The old lady leaned in further. "The bug you are seeking will not come easily; it is burrowed beneath the bark on the north side of the tree. You will need to claw it out. Just be careful it does not prick you with its horn, for its horn is highly poisonous."

Earth liked bugs as much as she liked other creatures. While she was fearful of many things unknown, she was not afraid of bugs, even poisonous ones. Earth took a little pot from the kitchen with a lid on it to capture the bug in, and set off into the woods to find the tree with the darkest bark.

Before long, Earth found the tree she was looking for. Its bark was several shades darker than the trees around it, with lumps spread around like warts. This did not look or feel like a friendly tree – a suspicion that would turn out to be true. As Earth climbed the tree, it creaked and groaned as if displeased it was being climbed. Branches that were conveniently placed to climb moved in the wind just out of reach as Earth made her way up the tree.

This was not going to be as easy as she had thought it might be. There was a creak above Earth's head, and as she looked up, a branch came crashing down towards her. She managed to jump out of the way, landing awkwardly on another branch to her left. If she was going to do this, she needed to do it quickly. Something inside told her that this tree was not going to let her up that easily. Digging all four claws in, Earth raced up the trunk, avoiding the branches that swooshed in an attempt to knock her off. No wonder the old lady didn't want to climb it.

Finally, she reached the top and made her way around to

the north side of the tree. Carefully she started removing the bark, piece by piece. She could hear a scurry of legs; the bug was trying to burrow deeper. She wouldn't have long until the bug disappeared for good. As she removed another piece of bark, a dark residue, like glue, clung to its host. There, inside the sticky substance, she could see the bug. It was a beetle, black and mean looking, with a horn on its head. She got the jar ready and placed it between the beetle and the bark. Using the lid, she peeled the beetle away, until it dropped into the jar, coated with the gooey substance.

Earth returned to the hut and handed the jar to the old lady. Without saying anything, the old lady took the jar, scurried over to the pot with the black substance and tipped the contents of the jar into it. With this, the contents of the pot came alive, wriggling and squelching. Out of the foul black substance emerged a bug equally as foul as where it had come from. A spike shot from its body and impaled the beetle, piercing its armour. Earth looked startled at what she was watching. The mouth of the foul looking creature opened wide, crunching its victim and swallowing it. Even Earth, who was used to bugs, found this quite disturbing.

She looked over to the old lady, who just looked back without saying anything at first. "Aren't you just a little bit curious about what you just saw?" the old lady asked.

Earth was curious. With all her knowledge she had not yet seen anything like this. Was this dark magic? What was it that ate the beetle and what was the concoction?

"I bet you are wondering what this curious bowl is," the old lady said, as if knowing what Earth was thinking. Earth nodded. "Well, it's called Gu. You could think of it as a kind of potion," the old lady said. "The beetle you brought to me was the missing piece. Now that there is only one bug left, I can complete the Gu".

"What is Gu?" Earth enquired with hesitation, not completely sure if she wanted to hear the answer.

"It can be used as a love potion, and it can be used as a poison. Time will tell," answered the old lady. "If you want some, it will be ready tonight."

Earth thought for a moment "I'm not sure I'll be needing that. And I really must get going now," she said, edging towards the door.

"That's right, you need to go and save your brother. You never know though; this potion could come in handy. It will be ready before dinner if you want to wait."

The old lady was right; it could come in handy, even if Earth was unsure as to why or how she would use it. Reluctantly, Earth agreed to stay until the potion was ready.

Just as the old lady had said, the potion was ready before dinner. Earth was now ready to leave, but her stomach had other ideas, as did the old lady. After several minutes of Earth trying to convince the old lady she really needed to go, she sat down to eat a delicious meal of bread, soup and noodles. As she slurped up the noodles, Earth couldn't remember seeing the old lady prepare the food. *That is silly, she thought, there's no way it could just appear!*

After the dinner, Earth thanked the old lady once again and made her way to the front door to leave. As she stepped out onto the verandah, a gust of wind blew past her head. Then the heavens opened and heavy rain poured down, creating pools of water within seconds.

"Come back in, you can't go out in that," the old lady said. "It's no good, you know, you'll have to stay another night."

Earth was starting to think she was never going to leave this place. Was this sudden storm the old lady's doing?

How could it be? She shrugged off the thought and made her way back inside.

The fire was roaring and Earth curled herself up in front of it, finally giving in to what she couldn't control. Moments later she had drifted off into a deep sleep.

Once again Earth was in a cave; the monster's rancid breath blew over her face. She ran as fast as she could, turning through one tunnel to the next, trying to find a way out. There, ahead of her, she could make out the light of an exit. She had to get there. With all her strength Earth willed herself forward, desperately trying to escape being caught by the creature. She ran to the opening, chased by the monster. As she got closer, the exit to the cave became smaller and smaller. Her heart pounded as she feared it would become too small to fit through. The moment she got to the exit, it was normal size again. She heaved a sigh of relief. There was really nothing to worry about. A flash of panic swept over her... *What about the monster, she thought?* She looked behind her, half-expecting to be eaten. There was nothing there. Just a big drop at the edge of the cave into nothingness.

Earth woke up – it was still dark; the sound of the forest was in full swing. Her heart was telling her to leave, her head was telling her to stay where she was, for fear of waking up the old lady. Confused by her feelings, Earth sat by the burning embers of the fire, wondering what to do next. She looked around the room for ideas. Something was wrong, something was missing. She looked around again to make sure. It was true, the old lady was not there. But where was she?

This is my chance to escape, she thought. Then she was gripped by fear again. What would she do if the old lady found her trying to escape? She needed a plan. *I'll creep out quietly, make no noise, watch my footsteps. If the old lady is there I'll tell her I heard a noise and came to investigate. That way the old lady won't think I was trying to escape.* Earth felt quite pleased with her plan. *What am I doing? I'm not a prisoner, I can leave when I want... can't I?* she thought.

Earth crept carefully and slowly to the front door. It was already open, but not enough for her to get through. As she gently opened it, it creaked, the sound magnified by the night. Her heart thumped against her chest. She waited a moment to see if she could see any movement outside. The moon was bright tonight and shone down like a torch. Nothing.

I don't like this, Earth thought. She made her way to the

edge of the forest, staying away from the path. *The path is too obvious; I'll be seen there.*

Earth continued into the forest, glancing over her shoulder now and again to make sure she wasn't being followed. No one was following her. She wasn't sure she liked this either; this was too easy. She had escaped the clutches of the old woman without a struggle. This was not like in her dream when escaping the creature. She was having doubts over whether the old lady was a creature at all. Perhaps she was just a lonely old lady who appreciated the company. Earth looked around again just to make sure though.

Walking deeper into the forest, Earth found a clearing with a dome-shaped shelter made of sticks. The dome was attached to the side of a large tree with a trunk at least five times wider than she was. The camp looked like it had been made recently.

I'd best be on the lookout in case the owner returns, Earth thought.

Nestling into the shelter, she made herself comfortable with a bed of leaves. Even with the thought of not knowing where she was, Earth felt cozy, warm and safe in the dome.

Tomorrow is another day. I'll set off at sunlight to find my brother.

The Heart Leads the Way

"Heart thinks, events materialize." - -Grandmaster Wong Kiew Kit

Sky was enjoying the rhythmic sound of drumming the tree stump. As each stick struck the stump it sent a vibration back up his arms. He felt connected to something beyond himself, and the more he played, the more connected he felt.

Before long Sky was lost in his playing, and his mind began to wander. At first, it was just thoughts and images of his father handing him the necklace that somehow was meant to protect him. Then his thoughts were of the wise old man. Sky could see him in his mind, perched on top of the rock, dispensing what seemed to be random and useless advice.

Sky chuckled to himself as he recalled the eagle flying over his head, desperately trying to convey an important message to him, whilst lacking the ability to talk as Sky could.

Then his thoughts turned darker. How foolish he had been in failing to notice the unsubtle gestures the eagle had made. How stupid he was in failing to immediately understand what 'finding nature's way' had meant. Sky's chuckle turned to a scoff.

Shrugging his shoulders, Sky chuckled once again and returned to his drumming. Yet, there was still something bothering him. Something that was nudging the back of his mind, and it wasn't the sound of the drumming. What was it the old man meant by "all you need to do is listen with more than your ears, and see with more than your eyes?"

Sky looked up to notice the hundred eyes that were looking back at him. He smiled in acknowledgment and continued drumming in the flow of happiness he was experiencing.

The creatures of the forest came closer – all except one, a beautiful creature he had not seen before. Its eyes shone brightly through the darkness of the trees. Sky looked in the direction of the creature to see if he could work out what it was.

The creature remained in stillness between the trees. Sky narrowed his eyes in an attempt to see more clearly, yet the more he tried the more the creature disappeared from sight. He knew the creature was still there though, as there was no sound or sign of it moving away.

Sky closed his eyes to listen. As he did, he could see the creature in his mind. He could feel the creature wanting to be there. Sitting there with his eyes closed, Sky had the feeling that what he needed was to listen with his eyes. He did not question how to do this; instead he slowly opened his eyes, and with a soft gaze he looked gently in the direction of the creature.

There, between the trees, Sky could see a glow of light surrounding this beautiful creature, radiating towards him. He closed his eyes again and bowed his head towards the creature, as if to say, "I am ready to listen, please guide me." The creature nodded back, tipping its head to reveal two horns.

Sky moved slowly towards the creature, keeping his head low. He knew he was in the presence of a divine creature that was rarely seen. To act rashly now would surely frighten the creature away. Sky's heart remained calm as he slowly approached. When he was a few feet away he stopped, once again bowing his head. He had heard stories of this great creature; he never thought he would actually meet one. This was Chi' Lin, a divine Unicorn, healer, helper and protector. Sky must have been on the right path, if he was blessed by the presence of Chi' Lin.

Chi' Lin looked into his eyes, and Sky felt his heart fill with joy. Chi' Lin nodded and turned to slowly walk away, appearing to be hovering just above the blades of grass beneath its hooves. Sky cautiously followed behind, keeping a little distance.

Feeling a little lost for words, Sky said the first thing that came to his head: "Thank you; without you arriving I think I would have been lost." Sky was being genuine; he really was feeling lost, although this might have been the first time that he would admit needing help.

Chi' Lin stopped. "You are welcome, Sky. I was drawn to your drumming; it spoke to me. I knew you needed help, and I will always help those who are destined for great things."

Sky was not sure how Chi' Lin knew his name, but then he realised as a celestial being she would know. But how did she know he was destined for great things though? Could Chi' Lin see into the future? What great things was he destined for? Was this why he was visited by Tianlong, the celestial dragon? Were all these things connected?

So many questions popped into Sky's mind that he wasn't sure what to think or ask first. Fortunately, he didn't have to as Chi' Lin could already tell what he was thinking.

"Your quest to find the divine peach tree must be followed through, Sky. There will be times when you feel it is too much. This will be the most challenging time for you, for it is then that you will feel like giving up. You must not give up. Follow your heart, don't fight against the nature of things, go with the flow and you'll find your way."

"I won't give up, I promise you," Sky replied respectfully. "Will you come with me, Chi' Lin?" Sky asked hopefully.

"I cannot, Sky. However, I will always be there when you need me most," Chi' Lin said peacefully, looking directly into Sky's eyes. Sky could not fully hide his disappointment, even though his heart had already given him the answer before asking.

"How will I know where to go?" Sky asked, looking a little vulnerable. "You do not need to worry, Sky, your path is already set in front of you. All you need to do is notice."

Sky now looked confused. He wasn't sure what it was he was supposed to notice and didn't want to look silly asking. He didn't need to, as once again Chi' Lin could read his expression.

"Just notice, Sky. Notice your feelings; they will tell you if what you are doing or where you are going is the right way or not. Notice the sounds around you; they will help lead the way. Notice light and darkness. Notice where colours become more vibrant. Notice unnecessary tension. Notice when you feel energised or overwhelmed. Just notice, Sky."

Chi' Lin fell silent, as if to give Sky time to absorb what had just been said. "Now you must go, Sky, trust yourself and that all will be ok, even when it seems like it is not."

Sky was grateful for the advice; it reminded him of listening to the wise old man who lived on the rock, only less cryptic. It now seemed like weeks, not days, since Sky had left his home in search of the Divine Peach Tree. As Chi' Lin left, Sky could feel some of his confidence leave him.

He stood there for a few moments without moving. He had mixed emotions about this trip. While admittedly a little anxious, he was also excited about finding the tree, the adventures he would have and what it would mean to him to achieve supreme wisdom once he had eaten the peach. The thought of him leaping high and jumping far with ease cheered him up. More than that, he noticed how he could change the way he was feeling with a simple thought.

He looked around him for signs of where to go next. To his left the trees looked dull and lifeless, to his right the trees look sinister, leaving Sky with a cold feeling inside. Looking ahead, Sky could see some light in the distance. He softened his gaze, as he had done before, and the light became brighter. *This is my path*, he thought. *This is the way.*

As he walked through the woods, he kept his focus gently on the light shining from the distance. Without really doing anything, he found his mind to be clear and fresh.

He started to notice the smells of the plants around him, the sounds of the birds in the trees, the crunching sound of the broken twigs and fallen leaves under his paws. He played with walking lightly, as if he was floating just above the ground like Chi' Lin. The sound of his steps became quieter, as did he.

This sense of inner peace was short-lived, broken by the sudden movement of something between the trees, only fifty metres away from where he was. Sky stopped in his tracks and looked around him. Nothing! He had the feeling that he was not alone. Was he being watched? There was another scurry low in the bushes, moving away from him. He softened his eyes, trying to catch sight of whatever it was lurking in the bushes. Nothing! He turned his head to the side with his right ear facing towards where the sound had come from. He heard a faint howl, followed by a yelp. Something was in trouble and he had to help.

Heading towards where the sound had come from, Sky leapt over branches, darted between trees, taking large strides on all fours to get there as quick as he could. As he got closer, his heart started to pound. There was another yelp, followed by several howls. Whatever it was, there was more than one. There was no time to think or be frozen by fear; he had to save this poor creature from whatever was attacking.

As he got closer he could make out the shape of a small pack of wolves, circled around a creature curled up in a ball in the centre of the pack. The wolves took turns to snarl, snap and growl at this poor frightened creature. Without hesitation, Sky accelerated his run, roaring as he bounded towards the pack. Charging at his target, Sky caught the first one unaware, sending it flying into the air. It landed with a heavy thud, letting out a yelp of pain. The others turned their attention from their prey to Sky.

One of the wolves sprang into the air towards him, teeth snarling. Sky stepped to one side and swiped the wolf with his paw as it narrowly missed him. The wolf landed awkwardly on its side and lay motionless, stunned from the strike. Sensing danger, Sky turned around to see two wolves slowly moving towards him, with their bodies low to the ground and shoulders poised to pounce. The two wolves circled around him, waiting for their chance to attack. Sky assumed his kung fu defensive pose at the ready. The wolf behind him snapped its teeth in the air in an attempt to break Sky's focus. Sky kept his eyes on both wolves. They crouched lower, edging forward, simultaneously pouncing towards him. Sky jumped backwards just in time for the two wolves to collide with each other.

Sky ran over to help the curled up creature on the ground.

It was a lion, like him. "Can you move?" he asked anxiously. "We need to get out of here, now. It won't be long until those wolves wake up again, and they won't be happy." Sky helped the lion up from the ground. It was hurt.

"Get onto my back, I'll carry you," he said with urgency. The lion pulled itself off the ground and climbed onto Sky's back. With the extra weight on his back, Sky could not run as fast as usual, but he knew he had to move as quickly as possible to get out of reach of the wolves. He looked around as he moved for signs of where to go next. In the distance he could hear running water. That's where he needed to head to.

Sky considered himself fit, however the fight with the wolves had used up a lot of energy, and now his legs started to feel heavy. *I need to stop*, he thought to himself. With the next intake of breath, he shook his head. I can't, *I can't stop now, the wolves will catch us.* After several more minutes of running through the forest, his legs felt like they were on fire. His muscles were aching and burning.

"I can't go on, we need to stop," he said to the lion he was carrying. With that, one of his legs buckled under the strain and he collapsed to the floor. His breath was heavy, and it felt like all the energy had been sucked from his body.

The two lions lay exhausted, supporting each other's bodies with their backs to a tree. "I'm sorry," Sky said, "I need to rest." Sky looked down to the floor to notice blood oozing out of his leg. One of the wolves must have caught him without him realising. Feeling ashamed of himself for giving up so easily, Sky's body collapsed into a heap. A paw gently stroked his forehead.

"It will be ok," came a gentle voice. "We'll be ok."

"Who are you?" Sky asked.

"My name is Earth."

"Pleased to meet you Earth. I am Sky," he replied.

"I can fix that for you," Earth said, looking at Sky's leg.

"That's ok, it'll be fine," Sky replied quickly, without hesitation. The thing was, Sky didn't really like asking for help, especially when he was hurt.

"Nonsense," Earth said sternly. "It will get infected if you don't do something about it."

Before Sky could reply, Earth had forgotten about her own pains from the wolves' attack and was off searching for a particular plant. A few minutes later she returned back with a few green leaves.

First she crushed and gently pressed the leaf to release a green juice. Rubbing the juice over the cut, the bleeding slowed down. Then she wiped the cut with the leaf to wash away any infection.

Placing the crushed leaf over the cut, Earth gave Sky some instructions. "Hold it in place Sky; after a few minutes your bleeding will have stopped and your cut will be healed."

Sure enough, after a few minutes the cut had healed. Sky was feeling much better and thankful that he had accepted Earth's help.

Sky sat upright as he was alerted to the sound of wolves approaching from a distance.

"We need to move Earth, now!" Sky said with urgency in his voice. "We can't hang around here, the wolves will catch us for sure. Let's go."

Earth nodded in agreement and they both got up and

moved quickly through the forest towards the sound of the water. It was getting louder, confirming they were heading in the right direction. Well, at least the direction of the water, that was.

Breaking through the thick of the forest, they both came to an abrupt stop at the edge of a chasm. They both looked at each other, confused. Sky was sure this was the way, nature had led him here. But instead of a nice gentle stream, they were met by a fifty-foot drop into a deep pool of water at the foot of a waterfall. The sound they could hear was the water crashing against the rocks as it fell to the pool.

There was no obvious river, just what appeared to be a bottomless pool. The sound of the wolves was getting closer. They felt trapped. Either they fought with the wolves again or they had to jump. Neither seemed like an inviting option.

The wolves broke through the trees and stopped several feet away. They looked really angry this time, drool foaming at their mouths as they snarled.

"I can't do this, Sky," Earth said, afraid. "I can't swim and I don't like heights."

"There's no choice, Earth, we have to jump. There are too many wolves this time, I can't fight them all."

They both looked down, back at each other and back at the wolves again. More wolves arrived. They had brought reinforcements this time.

"Grab my paw, Earth; we have to jump."

Sensing they were about to lose their prey, the wolves edged closer. The leader of the pack sprang forwards towards Sky and Earth.

"Now!" Sky cried out as he grabbed Earth's paw and dragged her into the air, before they plummeted into the pool beneath them.

The water engulfed them both as they were dragged down by the power of the swirl from the waterfall, forcing them apart, as the wolves stood staring, helplessly disappointed, into the water.

Sky was a strong swimmer, but as he fought against the force of the water dragging him down, he was spun around like a feather in the wind. Within a few seconds he had lost which way was up. Twirling around and running out of breath, Sky feared this could be the end, the end of his journey. It all seemed so pointless. With no more fight in him, he relaxed his clenched muscles and gave in to the water, letting it drag him down and down. His lungs were ready to burst and it felt like there was nothing more he could do. So he did just that, nothing. He closed his eyes, let out the last bubble of breath and accepted his fate.

A feeling of lightness filled his body, washing away his thoughts and tensions. Finally, he felt at peace. No thoughts, no worries, no tensions, nothing. He was happy. With his eyes still closed, he could see a beam of light like a beacon in the distance. The light warmed his heart and he could feel himself being pulled towards it like a magnet. Something had a hold of him.

Facing Fears

"With hope in our heart, we can find the strength to overcome fear."

Jumping from a great height into an abyss of water whilst being chased by wolves is not an ideal situation to be in – especially when you like all creatures enough not to want to bring any harm to them, have a fear of heights and a fear of water. Not a great combination when you consider the present circumstance Earth found herself in.

Earth could feel Sky tug at her as he leapt off the edge of the cliff into the abyss. She had no other obvious or immediate solution to her situation, other than to follow. As she hit the water, there was part of her that wished she had tried to stay and reason with the wolves. The same wolves that had, for no apparent reason or warning, attacked her, unprovoked, only a short while ago in the woods. Had it not been for Sky saving her, perhaps she would not have been here right now to consider the situation she was now in. But before she could think too deeply, her grip was torn away from Sky's as she was pulled deep into the water.

Unable to swim well, she looked around for something to hold on to. There was nothing. She tried to paddle her paws to find a direction. Unfortunately, the swirl was too strong. Realising that this was a wasted effort, Earth gave up trying so she could conserve her energy. She remembered her Papa teaching her how to relax her body and muscles when she was under pressure. She could hear her Papa's voice with her as she floated along with the undercurrent. It carried her effortlessly through a hidden tunnel deeper into the water. It was so much easier just going with the flow, instead of trying to fight against the power of the water.

Before long, the force of the water had carried her through a series of tunnels and into a small calm pool in a cave. A blue light shimmered softly off the walls of the cave, its reflection dancing on the surface of the water. Breaking the surface of the water, Earth took a large breath, only now appreciating the value of simply breathing. She sat soaked at a shallow edge of the pool against a rock, savouring each breath, as if it was amber nectar. She looked around the cave for an exit, but all she could see were the walls of the cave.

Sky! Where is Sky?! she thought as panic struck her heart. Sky was not with her. She had to find him. She looked around the cave in a desperate hope of seeing him, but all she could see was the shimmering blue light.

Without thinking, she jumped back into the water, putting her head under to see if there was any sign of him. Nothing.

She came back up to grab another breath before diving back down, this time using her paws to swim down deeper. A light from inside the tunnel where she had come from shone brightly, followed by the shadow of a creature. Without a thought, she swam towards it. Reaching out, she grabbed the first thing she could get hold of. It held back in response to her touch. Turning back towards the surface, she gave a yank; the creature followed. It was Sky.

Pulling Sky onto a rock at the side of the pool, Earth collapsed onto her back exhausted, letting out a sigh of relief that she had made it back up to the surface herself. Considering her fear of water, she had done well to jump back in at all. Yet, her instinct to help others in need was more powerful than her fear.

Sky was still not moving; his breathing was shallow. Earth asked him if he was ok, but he was unresponsive. She put her ear to his chest; his heart was still beating. She sat by his side, waiting for him to wake up. But as the hours went past, there was no sign of change. It was time to consult with her 'Book of Things' for a healing chant. As usual, she turned to the very page she needed:

Just as the water flows from the rivers to the seas, so may all beings receive your healing power. May they have the courage to overcome any obstacle. May their heart be filled with the joy of life.

May they follow the way of Compassion and Wisdom.

May they awaken from their sleep to bathe in your shining light.

Earth sat with her paws above Sky's body and repeated the chant a number of times. At the ninth time, a blue light glowed from deep in the centre of the pool. The surface of the water started to ripple as the light grew stronger.

Bubbles rose up into a luminous vapour that gently floated towards Sky, enveloping his body.

Sky opened his eyes, sat upright and looked at Earth, as if nothing had happened. "Did I miss something? After we hit the water it all went blank."

"Not much, Sky. Not much," Earth replied casually.

Sky looked down around his body, which was still glowing blue from the healing chant Earth had used to save his life.

"Why am I glowing?" Sky asked, looking around the cave for some clues.

However, it wasn't just Sky who glowed now; the walls and the ceiling flickered with a bright shining blue light. There was a rumble in the wall behind them and a few small fragments of rock tumbled towards the water near where they were sitting. The cave was moving, as if alive.

Sky got up to investigate. An opening in the wall appeared, revealing a passageway. They knew this was their only means of escape - that was unless they wanted to try and swim against the current, back through the tunnels from the pool to the waterfall. They headed cautiously to the opening.

"I don't like this, Sky," Earth said nervously. "I've got a bad feeling about this, like I've been here before."

"Don't worry, Earth," Sky said reassuringly. "I'm right here and I'll protect you."

Earth raised her eyebrows, as if surprised by Sky's unwavering confidence. Had he already forgotten that it was her who had just saved him? Perhaps he really didn't know. One thing was for sure though, if they were going to get through this then they needed each other.

"That's good to know," Earth replied. "Still, I think we should take it carefully through here, Sky, there is something not right about this."

"Really, I've got this, Earth," Sky said as the ground beneath his front paw crumbled away to reveal a large drop. Sky took a little jump back. "OK, I get it. I'll be careful."

They both jumped across the hole in the ground and landed safely on the other side. The passage led them on to a narrow ledge, forming part of a large, dimly-lit, open cave. It was a long way down. They looked around to see if there was any other way around this cave, instead of the narrow ledge they were on. To their right was a ridge. All they had to do was make their way along the narrow ledge and jump up onto the ridge.

Sky offered to go first, to test the way. As he edged along the ledge, he lost his footing on a loose piece of rock. The rock tumbled down and down. After what seemed to be forever, there was a 'clank' and 'thud' sound as the rock hit something solid. The sound echoed through the cave, bouncing off the walls and pillars. Sky looked over to Earth, giving her the 'I meant to do that' look. To him, this was all part of the adventure. You could say that he enjoyed the thrill of the danger.

As if he needed to impress Earth with his agility, Sky made a quick dash along the ledge and in one swift move leapt up onto the ridge. Earth was not so confident. Clinging to the rock face, she carefully edged along the ledge, making her way to Sky. He was perched ready with his paws to lift her up. The ridge formed part of a wider ledge, which proved to be a good enough place for Earth to catch her breath. This part of the cave was dark and made it difficult for either of them to make out where they should go next. Taking a few moments to think about what to do, Earth felt the urge to tell Sky something important.

"Sky, I need to tell you something before we go on," Earth said, catching his attention.

"Are you sure this is really the best place, Earth? If you hadn't noticed, we are stuck on a ledge in a dark cave. Shouldn't we be trying to figure out a way out of here?"

"It's important Sky, it's about why we are here, right now," Earth said, trying to give some sort of reassurance.

"I don't get you, Earth, what do you mean?" Sky said, looking confused.

"I dreamt it, Sky. I had a vision of being here before," Earth said.

"What do you mean? What was the vision?" Sky asked.

"I've been having a number of visions, Sky, and so far they seem to be happening. Not exactly like in the visions, but enough like the visions to make them real. That's why I need to tell you, in case we don't get out of here," Earth said nervously.

"What do you mean, in case we don't get out of here? What have you seen in your visions?" Sky asked.

"Don't you have visions, Sky?" Earth said defensively.

"Well, I have dreams, but I'm not the one telling you we won't get out of here," Sky said.

"Don't be angry at me, Sky, I'm just trying to tell you that in my visions I have been here before, and I wasn't alone. I was being chased by a monster. I'm afraid Sky," Earth replied, trying to control her own fears and frustration.

Realising that he was getting angry for no real reason, Sky tried to calm the situation down. "It's probably just a dream, nothing to worry about."

"I hope you're right, Sky; so far though they have come true – like the branch in the river, the old lady in the hut and me falling into the water and being pulled down," Earth said, as if Sky would know what she was on about.

"What do you mean, the branch in the river? I almost fell into the river because of a branch," Sky said, now quite excited to hear more about the visions.

"Well, in my vision I saw a branch floating towards me, as I stood by the river's edge looking for a way to cross. When the branch came close, I jumped on it and onto the other side of the riverbank. Later, when I actually came to cross the river, I waited for this branch to appear. At first it did not come, and I started to doubt my vision, but then it appeared. It was not quite so effortless as in my vision, however, I made it, thanks to the branch. What happened to you and the branch?" Earth asked.

"I was also looking for a place to cross the river. The wise old man in our village had told me to find nature's way and not to rush ahead. I saw a tree that had fallen over the river, so I crossed it. As I got halfway across the tree split into two main branches. So I took the one that I thought would be the most solid. Turns out that it wasn't, because it snapped, just before I jumped off, and ended up floating down the river," Sky explained.

"Perhaps it was the right branch you chose, Sky, for if you hadn't chosen that branch, perhaps I would not have crossed the river and met you. I have a feeling that it was meant to happen."

"Tell me about your visions, Earth. What else happened?" Sky asked, now starting to believe that, just maybe, there was truth in these visions.

"I also had a vision of an old lady who lived in a hut in the woods. There was also a monster with rancid breath that was chasing me. When I was lost in the woods, I came across the old lady in the hut. At first I thought she was the monster, but I was wrong. I judged her too quickly. Turns out she was a nice old lady who lived on her own. She did give me this though," Earth said, taking out the small pot of Gu.

"What is that?" Sky asked, turning up his nose.

"It's Gu; it's supposed to be a potion, only I'm not sure if it's for good yet or bad," Earth said.

"Then why have you got it?" Sky asked.

"I'm not too sure, Sky. The old lady gave it to me and said it might be useful," Earth replied.

"Well, if it's bad that means it could be bad news for us as well," Sky said, concerned. "What's it supposed to do, anyway?"

"The old lady said that it would be either a love potion or poison, time would tell," Earth said, matter-of-factly, as if needing to defend why she had kept it.

"I still don't get why you have it, Earth. Why would you want a love potion or something that could poison something?" Sky said.

Earth was noticing a feeling of annoyance rise up inside her. Not at Sky, but at the situation. They were stuck in a cave arguing about a silly potion with no real explanation as to why she had it. She tried to think logically why she had waited for and accepted the potion, but she still had no real answer. This was what was annoying her, that maybe she had unknowingly made a wrong decision about something.

"Well, it's not like I'm going to use it on you, is it!" Earth said.

"I hadn't thought you would, Earth," Sky replied calmly, even though he was taken aback by her outburst. "I was just curious, Earth, that's all. Nothing to get upset about." Sky decided to change the subject.

"How come you ended up in the forest anyway, Earth?"

Earth turned her eyes towards the ground, feeling ashamed about what she was about to say. "It's my brother, Sky, he's gone missing."

She gave a little look up and back down again as she let out a sigh. "He's gone because of me."

"How can you say that, Earth? I'm sure that's not true," Sky said in her defence.

"But I think it is, Sky. I kept pushing him away. One day he left upset. Then someone from the village saw him being taken. You see, it's my fault. And it's up to me to find him," Earth said, with a tear rolling down her cheek. "If anything happens to him, I'll be the one to blame."

"Then let me help you find him," Sky replied, without giving it much thought.

"I'm not sure that's such a good idea, Sky. This is something I need to do alone," Earth said.

"Come on, Earth, you don't believe that. Besides, we work well together. Anyway, you already said we were meant to meet," Sky said, with a smile on his face.

"I guess you're right, Sky," Earth said, looking up. "We do work well together."

"Then that's settled. All we need to do now is get out of

here," Sky said, looking around the dimly-lit cave for some answers.

They both sat there for a while, looking over to each other in the hope that one of them would have a solution. Sky was the first to get up and look around the ledge they were on. He carefully made his way to the edge to see if any paths were visible from where he was. Looking down, all he could see was darkness. To their right, the ledge continued for some way.

"I think we should continue along this ledge, see if there is a way down or out. What do you think?" Sky said.

"It's probably the best we can do right now. You lead the way," Earth said, feeling thankful for Sky's initiative.

Sky carefully moved step by step across the ledge until he came to a stop.

"I need something to light the way, Earth. It's getting too dark to see where the ledge goes. Have you got anything?" Sky asked.

Earth thought for a moment. "Let me consult with my book," she replied.

"Your book, Earth? It's too dark to read."

"Don't be so hasty Sky, this is no ordinary book. It has often shown me the way. Let's see if it will do the same now," Earth said, feeling confident in her book's ability.

She took a moment to run her hand gently over the cover, as if silently speaking to the book with her gesture. Letting the book gently open to its chosen page, Earth could make out a picture she had drawn of the moon reflecting into a lake. As she looked at the picture, the moon grew brighter, coming to life on the page. Sky couldn't believe what he was seeing.

"See?" Earth said, smiling. Her face gently lit by the beam of the moon from her book. "Told you it would work."

Feeling confident, she moved past Sky and made her way along the ledge.

"Look, over there," Sky said, pointing. "There's a tunnel. We need to get to it."

Earth nodded in agreement as they quickened their pace towards the tunnel. This sudden burst of energy and feeling of excitement was short-lived as they were interrupted by a large gap that lay between them and the tunnel.

"What do we do now?" Earth asked.

"We jump," Sky said, smiling.

"You've got to be joking, Sky, I can't jump that. It's far too wide," Earth said, with a worried look on her face.

"Nonsense," Sky said. "I'll show you."

Sky took several steps back to get a run up, looked over towards Earth and tilted his head before running towards the edge of the ledge. Earth dared not look as Sky's feet left the security of the rock. What happened if he fell? What would she do then? As she held her breath, Earth's heart squeezed in fear.

Sky on the other hand was doing what he loved to do, and that was jumping over big holes. His face lit up as he reached the point of no return. As he took flight his body became light. It was as if for those brief moments he could actually fly. He had heard of the kung fu masters who had mastered the 'art of lightness', giving them the ability to jump much higher than usual. Some, it was said, could become so light that they actually walked on water. And right now he was flying. Gently he landed down on the other side, turned on the spot with his paws spread out like a crane and looked over at Earth, who was still covering her eyes.

"Hey Earth, I made it. I told you I could," Sky called across joyfully.

"That's great, Sky," Earth said now looking up. "But how do I get across?"

"Don't worry Earth, I'm sure there will be something around here somewhere that can help you. Just give me a minute," Sky called back as he wandered off towards the tunnel. Sky had been gone for some time and Earth was beginning to worry he wasn't going to return for her. Had he been eaten by the monster in her dreams? Or worse, had he decided to leave her there and find his own way out?

A dim light flickered from the depths of the tunnel, growing brighter as it moved towards her. A large shadow with shapes like tentacles swung about as it drew closer. Earth took a step back into the wall of the cave. Fearing the worst, she waited for the monster to appear. But instead of a monster, Sky appeared, holding a flaming torch and an old rope dangling around his neck.

"Sorry I took so long Earth, it took me a while to unravel the rope. I guess we aren't the first ones to be down here. I'll throw one end of the rope towards you. Tie it around that rock sticking out of the wall just by you. I'll hold the other end and you can climb across."

"Are you sure that's a good idea, Sky? I mean, are you sure you can hold it while I climb across?" Earth said.

"Of course I can... I have a really strong stance," Sky said confidently as he threw one end of the rope over to Earth.

Earth tied her end onto the rock as Sky had instructed. Sky wrapped the other end around his waist and sank down into a deep kung fu stance, with his legs wide and rooted to the ground. Holding onto the rope, he called out, "OK Earth, I'm ready for you now."

"Don't you dare drop me, Sky, I'm trusting you with my life," Earth said firmly, as she edged towards the gap. As Earth climbed onto the rope, it drooped. "Sky!" she called out, gripping onto the rope.

"Don't worry, Earth, it's normal for the rope to sag a little with your weight," Sky said.

"What are you trying to say, Sky?" Earth said, giving Sky an abrasive glance.

"Don't be silly, Earth, just focus on getting across here. That's all. Just a few more feet left, Earth. You're doing really well."

Sky's attention was diverted as he looked up towards the ledge at what he thought was the outline of a large figure. It must have been the shadow of the light, he thought, as the flames flickered. Earth was now almost within reach when the sound of crumbling rock caused her to stop. The rock which the rope was tied to was breaking away from the wall. Earth looked at Sky for an answer.

"Quickly Earth, you've got to move it," Sky said, with urgency.

Looking back up towards the crumbling rock, the figure of a creature appeared with the end of the rope in both claws. It tugged at the rope, causing Sky to momentarily lose his firm footing.

"Don't look back, Earth, just jump. NOW!" Sky shouted out.

Ignoring Sky's request, Earth looked over her shoulder, and catching sight of the creature she gulped.

"I can't hold it for much longer, Earth, jump now!"

With this, Earth swung her legs towards Sky and let go of the rope. Fearing Earth was going to fall short, Sky let go of the rope and dived forward towards the edge. Earth's eyes widened as she too realised she wasn't going to make it. For a moment it seemed like she was suspended in mid-air. Then gravity took hold and she dropped. Reaching out in desperation, Sky swiped the air below the ledge. Catching on to something soft, he pulled up. It was Earth's paw. Scrambling up his outstretched paws, Earth made it up onto the ledge.

Looking across the gap, their eyes met the creature, who was standing at the opposite edge, looking back.

"Run.... run Earth!" Sky said, picking himself up off the ground and grabbing the lit torch. They both bolted towards the tunnel.

"Follow me," Sky ordered, making his way left as the tunnel split off into three separate tunnels. "I know the way."

Earth quickly followed close behind with the embers of the flame flickering past her eyes.

Coming to what appeared to be a dead end, they both stopped.

"Oh great, Sky, you've led us to a dead end," Earth said crossly.

Ignoring her comment, Sky looked up above his head. Sure enough, there was an opening up above them.

"Now we climb, Earth. And I suggest quickly. We don't know what that thing was."

"I think I do, Sky. I think it is the monster in my vision. Lead the way, please."

Sky scrambled up, grabbing onto a small ledge above him. His paw wedged into a crevice. Keeping his body close to the rock, he used the shapes in the rock face to make his way up with the torch in his mouth. Earth followed close by.

Reaching the top, they stopped for a few seconds to catch their breath.

"We need to keep moving, Earth. Follow me."

"I hope you know where you're going, Sky."

"Kind of, but I must be honest, I didn't get much further than where we are about to reach. Beyond that we are both as wise as each other," Sky said.

Earth just raised her eyebrows in response.

The tunnel opened out into an enormous cave with stalagmites standing up like a series of huge pillars. Wisps of clouds concealed the ceiling. The floor, hundreds of feet below them, was covered heavily with a blanket of green vegetation. In the distance they could see crystal clear pools of water arranged in the formation of a lotus flower.

"Isn't it beautiful?" Sky said, who was seeing it for the first time.

"You're right, it is. It's the most beautiful thing I have ever seen," Earth said, with a smile on her face.

"I think this could be the way out. We should go before the monster catches us," Sky said.

"Can't we just rest here a while, Sky? If the monster climbs up the rock, we'll hear him. Look, grab those loose rocks over there. We'll lay them at the top of the opening where we came up. If the monster tries to climb up he'll lose his grip on the rocks and fall."

"OK, Earth, I agree. And I also take back what I said. You are a lot wiser than me. You know, I never did get to tell you why I came on this adventure. If you are happy to listen, I would very much like to share it with you. Even if you think I'm silly," Sky said, feeling better for wanting to share his story with Earth.

"Sure, let's move these rocks over first. I would love to hear your story."

Working Together

"When we stop to listen, we can learn something we don't know."

Sky turned to Earth, "Thank you, Earth. I mean it. It's not often I get to talk about the things I love doing. Most think I am silly, I try to talk to my parents, but they are often too busy to really listen. I talk to the wise old man on the hill. I think he listens, but he often replies in ways I don't always understand. I talk to the dragon, Tianlong, in my dreams; he seems to understand me. So I just want you to know that I really appreciate you listening," Sky said, his heart feeling lighter.

"You talk to Tianlong?" Earth's face brightened.

"Yes, he comes to me in my dreams. That's why I'm here really. As you've probably guessed I LOVE jumping and climbing and doing kung fu. It's what I do. My Pa loves it as well; he does it with ease. Although he probably wouldn't admit it. I wanted to make my Pa proud and prove to him that I had great kung fu, that I was awesome at jumping and climbing. That's when Tianlong visited me in my dream. He told me to search out the Divine Peach. That's where I would find wisdom. He said I needed both courage and wisdom, because courage alone would lead me to foolish decisions," Sky said, realising the truth of what Tianlong had said.

"Do you think that is true, Sky?" Earth asked.

"I do, Earth. I know I have rushed ahead many times. Often I have a feeling of overwhelming excitement that just carries me off like the wind. Sometimes it works out okay. Other times it leads me to trouble. If I was wiser, then I would make the right decisions all the time and not get into trouble or do the wrong things."

"I'm not sure that's true, Sky. I consider myself quite wise. I'm not brave like you, but I often consider the outcome before I rush ahead. Sometimes I think about it for so long though that I miss the moment. But even though I try to do the right thing, not everything goes right all the time. It's as if sometimes, we are meant to do things wrong so we can learn from our mistakes," Earth replied, absorbing what she had just said.

"I hadn't considered it like that before, Earth. I think you're right though," Sky said, acknowledging Earth's wisdom. "What do you think the answer is?"

Earth thought for a moment before answering. "I don't think there is one answer, Sky. I think it is different for everyone. Before I came on this journey, I lived my life in fear of doing the wrong thing. I was afraid of so many things. Afraid of getting hurt. Afraid of looking silly. Afraid of people not liking me. I think I was afraid of showing who I was. So I shut myself away in my Book of Things. I collected information, thinking it would make me better than other people. I thought if I knew lots of things then people would think I was clever, and like me. Then I met you, Sky. You're so full of energy, you literally buzz. You are so confident that you make me believe I can do more. It's because of you I was able to face some of my fears. Around you, Sky, I feel I can be myself," Earth said with tears in her eyes. "I think we all have things to show, as long as we aren't afraid of showing them. As long as we aren't afraid of failing. I think we need to be ourselves. Not what other people think of us or think we should be."

Sky wasn't used to receiving such compliments; it made him feel funny inside.

"What about the monsters, Earth? What do they want to show? Surely, they just want to do us harm," Sky asked.

"It is true, Sky, that some monsters do want to do us harm. But that does not stop us asking why? Why do they want to do harm? What is it that they want to say? What is it that we need to understand? It's easy for you and me to tell each other how we feel, what we need and what we are afraid of. I don't think it is that easy for monsters. It must be hard to be a monster in this world," Earth said, feeling a little sorry for the monster that was chasing them.

"Are you not afraid of what the monsters will do to you, Earth?" Sky asked.

"Of course I am, Sky. I don't want to die. I'm not ready to die. Have you ever noticed how afraid the monsters are too?" Earth asked.

"I hadn't really stopped to think about it. But now you mention it I did feel the energy the wolves gave off as they readied themselves to attack," Sky replied.

"And how did that make you feel, Sky?" Earth asked.

"Afraid a little, at first. My heart raced. I became alert and ready to defend myself. It made me feel stronger," Sky answered. "But that's normal, isn't it?"

"Well yes, fear is normal. It helps us become alert. But don't you find it interesting? That when you thought you were in danger, you changed. You were ready to defend yourself from danger and it changed the way you felt. It gave you power. When I'm afraid I feel weak. I feel useless," Earth explained.

"Not from what I've seen, Earth. You dived into the water, even when you were afraid. You leapt from the rope when the monster grabbed it. I think you're brave," Sky said, in an attempt to make Earth feel better about herself.

"That's because you were there, Sky. You make me feel brave because you are brave," Earth replied, causing Sky to blush again.

"That's how we are different though. You seem to be able to turn your fear into something positive. I don't. How do you do it?" Earth asked hopefully.

"It's my kung fu training, Earth. It helps me feel stronger. It helps me focus. You could do it," Sky said.

"Would you teach me, Sky?" Earth asked. "I'm just a beginner, Earth, not a teacher. I could show you a few things though." Sky moved into a space to demonstrate.

"First you must be relaxed. Relax your muscles, relax your breathing. Then I start with this, it's called Lifting the Sky." Sky straightened his arms and raised them above his head, gently pushed up as if reaching to the sky, and then gently let his arms down to his sides.

"Then I do this, Pushing Mountains," Sky said, as he brought his arms up to his chest and gently pushed his paws out as if he was pushing something away. He repeated this movement several times.

"Then Separating Water." Sky changed his hands from Pushing Mountains to a movement like swimming.

"Then Gathering the Cosmos," he said, drawing his hands in a smooth circle from the sides of his body, over his head and down towards the ground. "You try."

Earth got up and copied the movements as Sky repeated them a few times.

"Excellent. Just remember to relax your muscles and breathe as you do them. It's this that helps you focus your energy," Sky told Earth.

Earth carried on repeating the movements until Sky instructed her to stop. "Now, just stand there and let your energy flow." Earth wasn't quite sure what Sky meant by this, but she did it anyway. Closing her eyes, she felt warmth gently flow over her body. It felt good. Opening her eyes, she smiled at Sky.

"Thank you," she said. "That feels good."

"It does, doesn't it? That is part of my training every day. Then I do this," Sky said as he moved into a wide stance, squatting down as if sitting on an invisible stool. "This is called Cloud Hands," he said, whilst circling his paws in front of his body. His movements were getting faster and faster, until they became a blur.

"I don't think I'm ready for that yet, Sky," Earth replied.

Sky jumped out of his stance, smiling.

"And you find this helps you with being brave?" Earth questioned.

"I think it helps. But that's not why I do it. I do it because I love doing it. It makes me feel good," Sky replied.

"Was it your kung fu that helped you know which way to go in the forest as well?" Earth asked.

"No," Sky said, shaking his head. "The wise old man told me to follow nature's way. Then I met Chi' Lin and she taught me how to see things."

Earth almost fell over where she was standing. "You met Chi' Lin as well? I dreamt of Chi' Lin. I had a vision I was in the forest when I heard drumming. As I moved towards the sound, I caught sight of Chi' Lin. That was you in the forest, Sky," Earth said, feeling gratitude.

"It's true, Earth. That was me. Chi' Lin taught me how to see with more than my eyes, to listen with more than my ears. It was this that led me to you." There were too many coincidences for Sky to deny. He turned to Earth. "It's as you said, Earth, we were meant to meet, this was supposed to happen. We are in this together, no matter what."

"No matter what," Earth said, smiling as she joined paws with Sky to seal the pact.

They both sat down, looking out into the vastness of the cave without speaking for several minutes.

"So what do we do now?" Sky asked.

"We need to find a way out of here," Earth said, looking for the best way to cross the huge cave. "But I'm feeling a little bad, Sky."

"What about?" Sky asked. "I'm thinking about what Chi' Lin told you. What Chi' Lin would do. She wouldn't purposely set out to hurt the creature. I don't think we should do it. I think we should take back the stones and then find our way out of here. What do you think?"

Sky thought for a moment. "I think you're right, Earth. Let's move them."

Dragging away the final stones, Sky and Earth moved over to look down to the place they had climbed up. As they peered over the edge, they came face to face with the creature as it reached the top. Its rancid breath reached their nostrils. Stumbling backwards in surprise, they landed in a heap on top of each other. The creature moved slowly towards them, its eyes bulging, mouth open wide, showing its large fangs.

Sky leapt to his feet, paws spread out to the sides as he stood between Earth and the creature. "What do you want with us?" Sky demanded, appearing unafraid. "Why are you chasing us?"

The creature closed its mouth, looked at Sky and then down at Earth. "I'm not chasing you," it said in defence. "I've been trying to catch up with you since you entered the cave. You move fast though."

Sky was confused. "If you're not chasing us, then why did you try and throw my friend off the rope?"

"Throw your friend off the rope? Oh no. I was trying to save you. But before I could your friend jumped off. If it weren't for you she would have fallen to her death. I'm sorry if I frightened you, but there was no time for introductions as the rock you tied the rope to was crumbling from the wall," the creature replied.

Sky lowered his paws as Earth got up and stood next to him.

"We thought you were trying to eat us. I thought you were the monster in my visions," Earth said.

"And did the monster in your visions cause you harm?" the creature asked.

Earth thought for a moment. "Well, no, it didn't."

"Then why did you run?" the creature asked.

"Because we thought you wanted to hurt us," Earth replied.

"I have no intention of hurting you. I'm here to help you. When I saw you both come out of the cave with the pool I knew you were the ones I've been waiting for," the creature said.

"What do you mean, you have been waiting for us?" Earth asked.

"I've been down here for a very long time," the creature replied. "Longer than I care to remember. I couldn't leave. Well, not on my own. After five centuries I got to know these caves well. There is no way out for me," the creature said.

Earth and Sky looked at each other and gulped. Sky turned

to the creature. "If you've been down here for five-hundred years, how are we supposed to find our way out?"

"I'm glad you asked. You're both going to help me," the creature replied.

"How are we supposed help? We don't even know these caves," Sky said.

"It's not how well you know the caves that matters. It's the skills you both came in with that matter," the creature said.

"And what makes you think we have some kind of magical skills that will work?" Earth asked.

"I don't," the creature replied. But before he could continue, Sky interrupted.

"Oh great. That's no help."

The creature waited patiently until Sky had finished and said nothing of the interruption.

"I mean, I don't think it is magic – your skills, that is. Both of you came into this cave with some very particular skills. You," the creature said pointing at Earth, "have a talent for sounds, plants, creatures and healing. And your book helps guide the way."

"How do you know all that? How do you know about my book?" Earth asked.

"As I said, I've been down here for a very long time. And in that time I have also learnt some particular skills. One of those skills is to be able to see into the future. So I knew you would both come."

"And what about me?" Sky asked eagerly.

"You have a gift of movement and energy. You have the ability to see, hear and sense things that others can't. Although your skills are not yet fully developed," the creature told Sky.

Sky was a little taken aback – not by the idea that the creature knew these things, but because the creature had suggested he still needed to learn more. But before Sky could say anything, the creature continued.

"We all have something to learn, me included. It does not matter how old you are or how many lives you have lived, there is always still more to learn. Fortunately, you are a quick learner." The creature gave a smile, baring its teeth.

Sky felt reassured, but also curious. "Can I ask how it is that you became trapped down here?"

"Of course," the creature replied kindly. "A few hundred years ago I became very greedy. So greedy that I did not know how or when to stop eating. The heavens were not happy with my behaviour, so made it that I could only eat gold. So I ate and I ate, more and more gold. When good people needed help I would help them. But when people were bad, I punished them. I then heard of this mountain. That it had all that I could eat. So I headed here. After I found my way in, the cave sealed. I was trapped."

Sky and Earth looked shocked.

"I take it that you won't punish us," Sky said.

"Unless you need it," the creature said jokingly.

"What is your name?" Earth asked.

"They call me Pi Yao," the creature replied. "And you are Sky and Earth."

"That's right," Earth replied, unable to hide her astonishment. Sky was now used to creatures knowing his

113

name, so it came as little surprise.

"I suppose you are wondering how it is I know all these things?" Pi Yao questioned.

Sky wanted to speak, but got beaten to the reply by Earth. "I am curious, Pi Yao. These last few days have been..." Earth paused. "Well, let's just say that they have not been normal."

"That's one way of putting it," Sky chipped in.

"I quite understand. For many, what you have been through could be quite frightening. But you have good friends protecting and guiding you. It's not every day that you get to meet Tianlong, Chi' Lin and me," Pi Yao said with a knowing look. "It is not by chance you have come to me. I saw you in my meditation and called to you. Earth was the one to see me, although her fear clouded what she could see. I knew that Earth would not be able to make it alone, just as you could not, Sky. But together you can."

Sky and Earth looked at each other. In their hearts they knew this to be true. Already, both had saved each other.

"So were the wolves your doing?" Sky asked accusingly.

"No, they had nothing to do with me. I just called you, that's all. I knew you could help me, just as I will be able to help you," Pi Yao said.

"How are you going to help us?" Earth asked.

"By showing you how to combine your skills."

Sky and Earth felt excited at the prospect of combining their skills. What would they be able to do?

"Let me show you," Pi Yao said, sensing Sky and Earth were eager to learn. "Sky, you have already been shown by Chi' Lin how to listen with more than your ears, to see with more than your eyes. You managed to do this in the forest. Now you must combine these skills. Close your eyes. Relax your breath. Let your breath guide you."

Sky opened his eyes to see what was going on.

"Keep your eyes closed, Sky. You must still your mind. Good, good," Pi Yao said reassuringly.

"Now, with your eyes closed, let your vision go out into the cave, just as you would if you were listening. Good, that's it," Pi Yao continued, sensing Sky was doing well.

Earth shuffled, not sure what she should be doing or when she would get to try. Her movement made a scraping sound, enough to distract Sky. Sky turned his head towards Earth, peeking a look.

"You must focus, Sky. Don't be distracted by what is around you. Let's start again. Close your eyes. Relax your breathing. Let your breath flow out into the cave. Good, good. Now let your vision go out into the cave, eyes closed."

Earth sat perfectly still, not daring to move. As she did, she felt the calm of the moment flow over her, easing her restlessness.

"Now let your hearing go out into the cave. Let it gently float out, like a ripple in a pond. Good. Now let your vision and hearing become one." Pi Yao paused for a while, allowing enough time for Sky to feel and experience the instructions. "What do you see, what do you feel?"

"I see the shape of the rocks, I see the edges of the cave, I see the plants and the trees," Sky replied.

"What else do you see?" Pi Yao asked.

"I can't see anything else," Sky replied.

"Try," Pi Yao requested gently.

"I can't. I can't see anything." Sky could feel himself getting frustrated.

"Calm your emotions, Sky, breathe," Pi Yao said.

"I can't, I can't do it," Sky said opening his eyes.

"It is not true, Sky. You can do it. You were doing it. But when we become angry or frustrated, it clouds our vision. The connection is lost. I'm sorry if I pushed you," Pi Yao said apologetically.

"It wasn't you, Pi Yao, it was me. I tried but couldn't do what you asked," Sky said.

"I will only say this once, to you both," Pi Yao said, closely examining both of their faces. "Any negative thinking will only harm you. It will slow you down. It is not what we can't do, but what we don't believe we can do that holds us back. Your parents, Sky, didn't believe you could make this trip, so they tried to hold you back. You, Earth, were afraid of coming, but you found your courage when you thought you would never see your brother again."

117

Earth's mouth fell open at this point. "I didn't tell you any of that. Do you know everything about us?"

"No, not everything. I can only see what is given to me. That's why I can't find my way out of here on my own. I was not meant to leave until I met you two. It was my destiny to show you both the way. So you could go on to do what it is you are going to do," Pi Yao said. "If you want to rest, we can. Another few hours or days won't change much for me."

"No, we want to carry on," Sky and Earth said together, looking at Pi Yao and then each other with a smile.

"Ok, so we continue. Earth, take out your book and turn to a clean page. Draw what you see," Pi Yao said.

"That's it, no special breath or vision, just draw." Earth must have sounded rather disappointed, as Pi Yao smiled and winked at her.

"That's it for now, Earth. Just draw what you see."

Earth studied the landscape of the cave for several minutes. She wanted to get a feel for what was out there before she started drawing. Thinking this was a test of some kind, she looked at every corner and crevice, every rock and tree, taking everything in. Whatever she was supposed to do, she didn't want to fail. *Did Pi Yao literally mean draw what I see? That would take forever* Earth thought to herself. She looked at Pi Yao and back to the cave, then back to Pi Yao again, hoping to pick up some kind of clue.

"Don't over-think it, Earth, just draw. It doesn't have to be a perfect picture of what is there, just what you see," Pi Yao said.

This was enough of an answer for Earth. She was over-thinking it. She wanted to get it so perfect that in her mind there was no room for anything else, including taking in what it was she was supposed to be seeing. So she looked again into the giant cave. Only this time she wasn't thinking about how to make the picture perfect or how she was going to impress Pi Yao. She just looked, really looked. Taking out her pencil she began to draw. As she did, the picture started to draw itself. The pencil moved with ease, without thought or interruption.

Looking down at the paper, Earth was surprised by what she had drawn. It was simply beautiful, as if alive on her page.

"Excellent, Earth. You have done very well," Pi Yao congratulated. "Now, please give the book to Sky."

"My book!" Earth exclaimed, holding onto it tightly.

"Yes, your book. Sky needs it to complete the task," Pi Yao replied.

"It's just... it's just that I don't usually let anyone hold my book. You see, it is very special to me," Earth said, trying to convince herself of why she shouldn't let Sky hold it.

"I know, Earth. It is indeed a very special book. Do you know why it is so special?" Pi Yao asked.

"Is it because of the Dragon scale?" Earth asked, trying to answer the question.

"It is, Earth, but do you know who that dragon scale belonged to?" Pi Yao enquired.

"No, I don't. I just found it in my valley, hidden under a stone," Earth said. "

Hidden... or waiting for you?" Pi Yao said, tilting his head.

"What do you mean, how could it be waiting for me?"

"I can tell you, Earth, that it was not there by accident. The dragon who gave that scale did so knowingly. Knowing that you would find it," Pi Yao replied. "Sky knows who it is, don't you Sky?"

Sky looked at Pi Yao and then at Earth. "It belongs to Tianlong."

"That's right, Sky. Tianlong gave one of his precious scales, knowing that Earth would find it. Knowing that Earth would find you," Pi Yao said.

"How do you know this?" Earth asked.

"Because, Earth, we are all connected," Pi Yao replied. "And it is because of this that I ask you to hand the book to Sky."

Earth looked up at Sky, loosened her grip and placed it carefully into Sky's waiting paws. "Please be careful with it."

Sky looked at Pi Yao, not sure what he should now do.

"Open the pages to the drawing, Sky," Pi Yao instructed. "Close your eyes again as you did before. Focus gently on your breath. Let your vision and hearing become one. Bring the feeling of what you see inside of you. Good, good. Now let it flow onto the pages." Pi Yao signalled to Earth to look at the page.

A swirling light moved around the page as if searching. Finally, the light settled on a chosen path that meandered across the page, highlighting the way.

"Open your eyes, Sky. See what has been revealed," Pi Yao instructed.

The Changing Path

"Your feelings are yours alone, so choose them wisely."

S ky and Earth sat staring at the page. This was not the first time the book had revealed something hidden. But it was the first time it had responded to someone else.

"So this is it. This is our path, Pi Yao," Sky said.

Pi Yao looked pleased with the results and nodded. "You have done well. Both of you."

"So let's go, what are we waiting for?" Sky got up, taking Earth by the paw.

"Wait." Pi Yao stopped them from moving. "I have to warn you. This is not as simple as just following the path in your book. The path will change as we move."

"What do you mean, the path will change?" Earth asked.

"I mean the cave changes. Trees move, as do the rock pillars," Pi Yao replied.

"How is that even possible?" Sky asked.

"In the forest, Sky, I climbed a tree that did not want me there. So it moved, it groaned and it tried to knock me off," Earth warned.

"Earth is right, Sky. In this cave, anything is possible. You saw how the light in the first cave you entered created an opening. How the rock you tied the rope to gave way. There was no way that rock was crumbling away before," Pi Yao explained. "We need to be careful, not rush ahead," he said, looking at Sky.

"So how do we do this?" Earth asked.

"You'll need to keep your book open, Earth. Sky will lead the way, slowly. He will use his skills to look and listen out for changes. If I say stop, stop. If I say run, run," Pi Yao warned. "Do you understand?"

"We understand," replied Earth.

Pi Yao turned to Sky, waiting for a reply. "I understand."

"Okay. This means, Sky, that you'll need to stay aware all of the time. You must stay relaxed, whatever happens. Once we step down there, anything can happen." Said Pi Yao.

"You make it sound like the cave will try and stop us leaving," Sky said.

"That's exactly what I am saying. So are you ready to leave?"

"Absolutely," Sky said for the both of them.

Earth held her book open, carefully surveying the page as they slowly made their way down a path, taking them deeper into the cave. Sky focused on his breathing, keeping it relaxed as he moved, extending his hearing and vision further into the cave. The path on the page hadn't changed since leaving the safety of the ledge.

"So far, so good," Earth whispered.

"Don't be fooled. I've tried many times to escape through here. And failed as many times," said Pi Yao.

"Ah, but you didn't have us," Sky said.

"Stay focused, Sky, you can't afford to lose focus, not even for a moment," retorted Pi Yao, glancing across to the book as they moved. "Stop," he ordered. "Your book has changed, Earth, the path has changed."

"Where?" Earth asked.

"There," Pi Yao said, pointing down at a point several feet from where they were standing. "Your book will show it before we see it, Earth. We need Sky to stay really alert. He needs to read the changes. See them, feel them, hear them. Look for changes in colour, Sky, changes in sound."

"I'm trying, I really am," Sky said.

"I know you are, Sky. Let me show you what the change is on the path we just saw in the book," Pi Yao said, carefully moving towards an area of ground in front of them.

"I don't see anything," Earth said.

"Not yet you don't. Sky, look there," Pi Yao said, pointing

to the ground.

Sky softened his gaze as he had done in the forest. The ground had a hole in it at least five feet wide. He carefully moved to its edge and looked down, unable to see how far it went.

"I still don't see it," Earth said.

"You're kidding, right?" Sky said, surprised. "Are you telling me you can't see this great big hole that I'm standing next to?"

"No I can't," Earth said. "I really can't."

"Look," Sky said, picking up a rock and throwing it into the hole. From what Earth could see, the ground just swallowed the rock up.

"What just happened?" Earth asked with a worried look on her face. "The rock just disappeared."

"Yes, disappeared down the hole," Sky said "You really don't see it, do you?"

"No, I don't." Earth replied. "Why can't I see it?"

"Because the cave conceals itself. It doesn't want you to see it, so it hides in the open," Pi Yao said. "It appears to be friendly, but really it just wants to consume you. From this point on I need you both to use your skills to the best of your ability."

Moving around the hole, Sky led the way, once again focusing on his breath and senses. With sensitivity and awareness, Sky used his kung fu stances to test the ground as he walked, whilst scanning the surrounding forest for any changes. Pi Yao followed at the back. Earth whispered out instructions on which way to turn to stay on the path. Sky took in the information, which happened to coincide with his own intuition.

Carefully, they forged their way through the forest towards the rock pillars. Sky paused in his tracks, holding up his paw to signal for the others to stop. Waving his hand gently to the ground, they crouched.

"What is it?" Earth asked.

"Wait," Sky whispered back, keeping his hand up as a warning. After a few minutes Sky turned to them both. "I saw something, it moved liked a shadow through the trees over there."

"The shadow spirits are hard to detect. You did well to see it," Pi Yao said.

"What are they?" Earth asked.

"They are the people and creatures that became trapped down here and never found their way out. Now they are stuck between our world and the next," Pi Yao explained.

"Are they dangerous? Can they hurt us?" Earth asked as Sky continued to survey the area.

"If we cross their path and get in their way, then yes, they can hurt us. But they won't seek us out," Pi Yao answered.

"We have another problem," Sky alerted them. "The rock towers are about to move and they are our path."

"Then we need to move quickly. Sky, lead the way and fast, but keep a look out for any further changes," Pi Yao ordered.

Quickening their pace, they made a dash for the rock pillars. Like convenient stepping-stones, they temporarily aligned. Leaping from one step to the next, they made their way up to the tallest pillar. When they reached the top, they realised the gap between them and next pillar was too far. The pillars below had already started to move away as well.

"What do we do?" Earth asked frantically.

"Give me a moment," Sky requested.

"We might not have a moment," replied Earth.

"Let him do his thing, Earth. Give him a moment," Pi Yao suggested.

"There," Sky said, pointing. "Check your map. You should see a platform appear in a few seconds. We won't have long because it's going to move. But we'll have long enough to jump onto it and onto the other pillar. Do you see it?"

"I do," Earth replied "I see it on my map, but not where you're pointing."

"Don't worry about that, just trust me and jump when and where I do. Ready... it's about to come," Sky said, taking a small step back before he ran and jumped into an empty space between the pillars.

For a second he disappeared down into the gap. "Now!" he

shouted. "Jump now!"

Pi Yao and Earth jumped onto the platform as it appeared. "Jump again." Sky ordered, and before they could think, they were leaping across to the next pillar.

"We'll be ok for a few moments," Sky said reassuringly. "But then we need to move again."

"Move where?" Earth said, looking around her for some answers.

"From now on, Earth, you are just going to have to trust me." "Follow me," Sky said, walking off to the edge of the pillar. As he reached the edge, he gave a little glance back and smiled. He was loving it. "Let's go," he said, lifting his leg up just in time for a step to appear, followed by another and then another.

"You 'll need to move quickly," he said. "They won't be around for long, keep up and keep an eye on your book."

Looking down at the book whilst trying to step up a series of moving steps was a challenge in itself.

"Move to your right," Earth called out.

"I see it, thank you," Sky said appreciatively as the step he was about to tread on shifted to the right towards an opening above them, but stopping just too short for them to step up.

"I'll jump up there, then catch you, Earth," Sky said, leaping up onto the ledge above.

"Let me help," Pi Yao offered as he lowered his paws for Earth to stand on.

Lifting her up, Sky reached out and grabbed her paws, pulling her up onto the ledge.

"What about you?" Earth asked.

"Step back," Pi Yao instructed as he leapt with ease to the ledge.

"Impressive," Sky said, in admiration.

"I may be old, Sky, but I still have a few tricks left in me," Pi Yao replied.

"I never doubted you," Sky said, smiling for a moment before focusing on his surroundings.

Having reached the ledge, the three of them headed into the tunnel, hoping to find a way out. Earth had a strange feeling in her chest, alerting her to danger.

"I don't like the feeling of this. It feels wrong, we shouldn't be in here," Earth said, with a tremble in her voice.

"Nonsense, Earth, this is the way your book led us, it must be the way," Sky replied firmly.

"I'm just saying Sky that this feels wrong. What do you think, Pi Yao?" Earth asked.

"This is not up to me. You need to choose. If you want to go back and try to find another way, then choose. If you want to stay on this path, then choose. Either way you must be the ones to choose. Remember, I've been waiting for you to lead me out of here. Now lead," Pi Yao said.

"Check your map, Earth. What does it say?" Sky asked.

Earth looked at her 'Book of Things'; the path had not changed course. However, there was something new. It looked like a small beam of light starting to shine through the page from further down the tunnel. The light was coming and going. Earth looked at it, waiting for it to do something else, hoping it would give her an answer to which way they should go. But it just kept appearing and disappearing.

Sky waited a while and then spoke: "So what does it tell you?"

"There is a strange flickering light at the end of this tunnel. It comes and goes. But the map still shows the path is this way," Earth replied, shrugging her shoulders.

"So we go this way," Sky said.

"Okay, but I'm still getting a weird feeling about it," Earth warned.

"You're probably just nervous and excited at the same time," Sky said, trying to reassure her.

"Do you think?" Earth said.

"Sure. Don't worry about it. We've done all right so far, haven't we?" Sky answered.

Earth raised her eyebrows and started walking down the tunnel, looking around her as she did.

"Sky," Pi Yao called out to get his attention. "We're not through yet, Sky. Don't lose focus. You still need to tune into your surroundings. Look and listen out for any changes. If Earth says she has a strange feeling about this place…" Pi Yao paused. "Then we should listen to that."

Sky slowed down his breathing, relaxed his body and let go of invading thoughts, his mind gently becoming clear, his senses tuning into any changes in sound, movement or colour. As he looked around, the walls of the tunnel gave a gentle buckle, as if coming in and out of focus. He shook his head, to make sure it wasn't him, once again tuning in to his surroundings. The ground gave a little moan and creak, undetected by Earth and Pi Yao. He looked at them to see if they had heard anything, but they just carried on, slowly walking as if nothing had happened.

Earth stopped. "I think I remember what it was now. What it was that feels weird. You know I told you about the dreams and visions. Well in one of those dreams a rancid monster…" Earth stopped to look at Pi Yao and softened her eyes. "Sorry Pi Yao, I don't mean you. In my dream I was being chased, chased down a tunnel. I could see the end of tunnel, the light from an opening. But as I got closer the exit became smaller and smaller. I think this is the tunnel."

"So what happened?" Sky asked.

"As I reached the exit it was fine, normal size. I stepped out onto a ledge with a thousand foot drop below me." Earth said.

"So it was ok then," Sky said, smiling.

"I guess so. But my dreams and visions are never exactly as they happen. I think we should be careful," Earth cautioned again.

"I am being careful," Sky said defensively. "I'm looking and listening, for everything and anything. If it moves or changes then I'll see it."

"I know, Sky. I'm not saying you're not being careful. I just wanted to let you know how I was feeling. That's important, right?" Earth said, feeling like she needed to explain herself.

"You don't need to explain it, Earth, I get it," Sky said abruptly.

Pi Yao could sense the tension building and decided to step in. "I need to stop you. This is not you doing this.

The tunnel has a hold over you. It draws out any negative feelings or fears you have. If you continue, you will say something you regret. Don't let it consume you."

"Why doesn't it affect you, Pi Yao?" Earth asked.

"I've been down here for a very long time. In this time, I have learnt how to control my feelings. Notice them, but not react to them. If you react to them then this cave will hear them and react back. I ask you both to relax, to stay calm."

"I'm trying to, Pi Yao, but it's really hard when you're being blamed," Sky burst out without thinking.

The walls and ceiling rumbled in reply.

"No one is blaming you, Sky. We are all here to help each other. If you feel emotions bubbling up and becoming overwhelming, then pause. Wait a moment, let out a breath. Just as you see the energy around you, so can you feel it inside you. Any disturbances in your thoughts or emotions are felt at many levels. This tunnel feels them. We don't want to upset this tunnel," Pi Yao said very calmly.

"I'm sorry, both of you. I'm sorry," Sky said.

"Okay, it's okay. Just gently focus again, Sky, on what you see and feel. Tune in to what is happening, but don't let the tunnel take charge of your feelings. They are yours and yours alone," Pi Yao encouraged.

Sky closed his eyes and gently focused on his breathing. He turned his head to one side and let his hearing penetrate the walls of the tunnel. The tunnel could sense his presence inside and tried to close him off. It felt like he was being squeezed out of the rock. He backed off for a moment. With his eyes closed, he allowed his vision to scan the tunnel. There was indeed a way out. A light reached back, confirming what he was sensing.

"There is a way out," Sky said gleefully. "But I have a feeling the tunnel isn't going to like it. I suggest we move quickly, but cautiously."

Earth and Pi Yao looked at Sky approvingly. Not just because Sky had found a way out, but because he wasn't rushing ahead, as he often did.

If Sky had been completely honest and upfront with Pi Yao and Earth, he would have told them that he was unnerved by what he had experienced a few moments before with the tunnel pushing back against his awareness. Despite all the things that had gone on, he wasn't sure how or if he should explain it. Instead, he thought it best to press on and find their way out.

Within a short while they could all see the dim light from the end of the tunnel. But something was wrong. It wasn't a constant light as it should be with an opening to a tunnel. It came and went. Either something was blocking it or it was playing tricks on them.

"Sky," Earth said quietly, "are you sure what you saw was the end of the tunnel?"

This time Sky remained calm. He paused for a moment, staying silent, as if listening out for something. "It is definitely an opening to the outside. But something is not right. It keeps opening and closing. I think what you saw, if your dream Earth was right, I think the tunnel is trying to stop us leaving."

"Then we move now," Earth said, quickening her pace into a run. Sky and Pi Yao followed, trying to keep up with her speed. Sky hadn't seen Earth run this fast before, but he too was fast when he wanted to be. He took a deep breath, pushed down his feet and sprung into a gallop. Pi Yao followed a small distance behind.

They could see the light of the exit. If they kept with this pace they would reach it within a minute. That's if the tunnel would let them. The ground began to rumble and move beneath their feet. Lumps and rocks appeared from the ground, trying to trip them up. But they were too nimble and avoided them. The tunnel was not happy. The ceiling began to crack and shift. It was coming down. Fragments of rock started to fall around them. One caught Sky on the shoulder as he tried to avoid it. Brushing it off, he continued to bolt towards the exit.

The light continued to come and go. The exit to the tunnel was closing. As they approached the exit, they knew little time was left before they would be trapped.

Glancing over her shoulder, Earth could see Pi Yao trailing behind. "Hurry Pi Yao, we need to hurry," she called out in desperation. But Pi Yao was going as quickly as he could for his age.

Another large chunk of the ceiling came crashing down, causing Sky and Earth to jump out of the way. The floor erupted, throwing them off balance. Getting to their feet, they ran faster towards the exit. The walls rumbled in protest, throwing fragments of rock in their path. Sky tried his best to maintain focus, but with all the noise he found it difficult. His instinct told him to run as fast as he could.

There was a large crashing sound behind them. The ceiling of the tunnel had collapsed completely. Pi Yao was either trapped behind the fallen ceiling or had been crushed. Either way, there was nothing Sky or Earth could do about it, and they knew it. They continued to run as fast as they could to the closing exit. But unlike Earth's dream, the exit did not return to normal size as they got closer, it continued to shrink. Another twenty seconds and they too would be trapped.

"Grab hold of my tail, Earth!" Sky shouted.

Earth had no time to question, she just did it. A second later the ground dropped away. Sky leapt with all his energy towards the now very small exit, spiralling in the air. Holding onto his tail, Earth followed.

Landing roughly on the other side, they skidded through on their backs towards the edge of the mountain ledge. Sky dug his claws into the ground to stop himself falling. Earth continued to slide past him. He reached out with his other paw to stop her, but she was moving too fast. In what seemed to be slow motion, their faces passed each other, eyes wide open in horror of the imminent doom. Earth tried desperately to dig her claws into something, but it was no good. She slipped over the edge and disappeared through the hovering clouds into the thousand-foot drop, her cry for help echoing through the valley.

Sky hurried to the edge, hoping she would still be there, somehow clinging to an overhang or bush. But she was gone.

"Noooooooooo!" He screamed out. "Earth..."

She can't be gone, he thought, *she just can't.* He was supposed to protect her, to keep her safe. They were meant to venture together. How could this be? Gone!

Nothing Will Pass with Ease

"Wisdom awakens, when you use what you know wisely."

S ky turned over onto his back. What was the point in going on? What was the point in finding wisdom if he had no one to share it with? Earth was his friend. A tear rolled down his cheek. His heart filled with pain.

"Woahhhh" came a distant sound. Sky got to his feet and looked over the edge of the mountain, just in time to see the head of a dragon burst through the clouds with something riding on its back. It was Earth, gallantly riding Tianlong.

143

Tianlong hovered level with the ledge. Sky stood speechless with his mouth wide open.

"I bet I had you worried there for a moment," Earth joked. "Had myself worried too. Thought I had met my end."

"No kidding. I didn't know what to think, what to do. I'm sorry. I should have grabbed you," Sky said apologetically.

"Yeah, you should have. Just kidding, Sky," she added as she saw the look of shock on his face. "It's not your fault. There was nothing you could have done. Anyway, our friend was watching us all of the time. There was no way he was going to let me or you die."

Sky breathed out a sigh of relief.

"So... are you going to jump on or what?" Earth asked.

"Too right I am," Sky replied, jumping on to Tianlong behind Earth. Holding onto Earth's waist, Sky gave her a little squeeze of appreciation. No words were necessary; she knew what he meant and smiled in reply.

"Upwards," she commanded. Tianlong nodded, stretching out his neck as they rocketed up towards the top of the mountain. The acceleration and speed was like nothing else they had ever felt. It was incredible. Tianlong flew close to the rock face to add effect to the speed and danger.

Landing on top of the mountain, Tianlong lowered his body to let Sky and Earth jump off. Looking all around, they stood in awe of the landscape. The views were nothing short of stunning. On a clear day like this, they could see for a hundred miles in each direction.

"Are you ready to find wisdom, Sky?" Tianlong said.

"I am, I am," Sky replied with eagerness. "Earth, would you check your book to lead the way?"

"I don't need the book, Sky."

"You mean you too have the gift of sight," Sky said, looking pleased.

"No Sky, I can see with my own two eyes. The peach tree you've been looking for is right over there. Tianlong brought us right to it, didn't you?" Earth said, looking for Tianlong. He had gone, without a sound or a goodbye.

"He does that, Earth," Sky said unsurprised.

Tianlong had brought them to one of several pillars of rock that formed the top of the mountain. The long grass disguised the edges and the size of land they were on, giving the appearance of one large mountain top. Sky and Earth ran in eagerness in the direction of the peach tree, coming to an abrupt stop at the edge.

"I think we have had enough falling off mountains for one day, Earth," Sky said. "Perhaps I shouldn't rush this part; we have come this far. I need to get across to the other pillar."

"Er, Sky… I don't know if you have noticed, but that pillar isn't joined to anything. It's floating."

"So it is, Earth. I think I can jump it though."

"Are you sure that's a good idea, Sky?"

"Unless you have a better plan, I think it is the only way," Sky replied, backing up so he could get a run-up.

Running at full speed, Sky waited until the last moment to jump and leapt into the air. Halfway across, he hit something hard, bouncing him back towards where he had jumped from. Rolling head over heels backwards, he stumbled to his feet with a confused look on his face.

"That was odd. Not the way I thought that would go," he said to Earth, looking perplexed. "I'll just run faster and jump higher."

Before Earth could stop him, Sky was up on his paws and running at full speed to the edge of the rock. With a look of determination, he sprung into the air towards the floating pillar with the peach tree. But just as before, he rebounded off an invisible wall of energy blocking his way. Rolling backwards, he landed on all fours.

"OK, so that didn't work," he said sarcastically.

"You really thought it would be that easy, Sky? After all we have been through?"

"No. Not really. But it was worth a try," he said, smiling. "Do you have any ideas?"

"Well, you could close your eyes and see what you can see," Earth suggested.

Sky did as Earth advised. He closed his eyes, relaxed his breathing and let his sight go out towards the floating pillar. But unlike before, the picture he saw in his mind was all foggy. He shook his head, trying to clear it. When he returned, the image was still foggy. Opening his eyes, he told Earth what he had seen.

"Can you consult your book, Earth?" Sky said hopefully.

Earth opened her book to the page with the map. Sure enough they were on it, standing on top of a pillar on the mountain. Next to them was a floating pillar. Some words faintly flashed up and then disappeared. *Look for a sign.*

"It just said look for a sign. There was nothing more than what we can see now," Earth said disappointedly.

Looking around, Sky spotted a flat rock jutting out of the ground, concealed by the grass. Pulling away the grass, he saw some writing.

NOTHING WILL PASS WITH EASE

"Well that's just great!" Sky said, frustrated. "We come all this way only to be told nothing will pass with ease. I could have told you that. Everything has been a struggle."

Sky could feel he was getting angry and decided to focus

on his breath to calm himself down.

"Don't worry," Earth said reassuringly. "We'll figure it out. Read it to me again."

"Nothing will pass with ease. Nothing will pass with ease," he repeated. "Any idea?"

"Not yet," she replied. Sky strolled around, pausing to say something, then realised there was nothing to be said. He sat on the edge of the pillar, gazing across to the peach tree. It was so close, almost within his grasp, yet he was unable to get it.

He thought about the wise man's words. The advice Tianlong had given him in his dream. What Chi' Lin and Pi Yao had taught him. But the answer still eluded him.

"Maybe," he said turning to Earth, "maybe, if nothing will pass with ease, then it will pass with an effort. Maybe I just need to really attack it. Really run at it like I have never run before. I remember my Pa telling me to just jump if I wanted to jump further. And the wise old man telling me it was what came before the jump. Perhaps I was too scared of falling so held back. This time I won't hold back. I'm really going to go for it."

Earth's reply did not come quick enough. Sky leapt to his feet, gathered the cosmos a few times to get extra energy, and in a cloud of dust sped towards the edge. He leapt fast, hitting the barrier as before. This time though, it absorbed him like a sponge. He felt like he was going to break through. But instead, it spat him back out at the same speed at which he had approached it.

Getting up off the ground and dusting off, he looked confused. "I don't get it Earth. Why can't I get through? The stone says that nothing will pass with ease, so I tried harder. Maybe I need to leap higher and run faster still."

"I don't think that's the answer, Sky. Why don't you take a minute? Come sit with me. Tell me again what you have learnt so far. Perhaps together we can work this out," Earth suggested.

"OK," Sky said, sitting down on the warm grass next to Earth. "First I asked my Pa how I could jump further. He said, "That's easy Sky, just jump." Next I asked the wise old man on the rock; he told me, 'It is not how you jump, but what comes before you jump.' He also told me all I needed to do was *listen, with more than my ears, and see with more than my eyes.*"

Earth sat quietly and listened.

"Tianlong came to me in my dream and told me *I have much courage, but without wisdom courage alone can lead to foolish decisions. That I needed to find wisdom to find my answer, and I would find it at the Divine Peach Tree.*" Sky paused for a moment and tried to recall what else he had been told.

"The wise old man also told me to *follow nature's way.* That led me to finding Chi' Lin. Chi' Lin told me to *notice. Notice my feelings, notice the sounds around me, they would help lead the way.* Also to *notice light and darkness. Notice where colours become more vibrant. Notice unnecessary tension. Notice when I feel energized or overwhelmed.* To not worry. To *follow my heart, to not fight against the nature of things.*"

"And that's all helped, right?" Earth said, nodding her head in agreement with what she was saying.

"Well, yes, it has. It has helped me to focus better and tune in to lots more than I could before."

"Is there anything more you can remember?" Earth asked.

151

Sky sat quietly again and closed his eyes for a moment, letting his mind become quiet, free from any distracting thoughts, waiting for the answers to come.

"Pi Yao taught me how to combine my skills. To focus and let my breath out. To *calm my emotions by focusing on my breath*. Ah," Sky said, realising something important. "Pi Yao was very clear about this. He said that *any negative thinking will only harm us. It will slow us down. It is not what we can't do, but what we don't believe we can do that holds us back*."

Sky sat for a moment in silence to absorb what he had shared. He turned to look at Earth. "What do you think?"

"I think you have a lot of useful things there, Sky. If you ask me, I would say the important things in what you have been taught are *not to worry, to listen, to notice and to go with the flow – nature's way*. Does that help, Sky?"

"I think so," Sky replied. "Let me have a look at what the rock says again, Sky," Earth said, examining the words. "Nothing will pass with ease. Nothing will pass with ease. 'Nothing' WILL pass with ease."

Earth looked up. "I think I've got it, Sky. NOTHING,

WILL pass with ease. You need to become *nothing*, Sky."

Sky looked confused. "How do I become nothing?"

A thought came to Earth as she took out her 'Book of Things'.

"I remember I came across a passage in my book, Sky, about *nothing*. It didn't make much sense at the time, but it seems important now."

Flicking through the pages, Earth paused. "Here it is, I'll read it to you -"

Let go, let go, let go Until there is nothing. Nothing to do. Nothing to let go. Nothing.

"Does that make sense to you, Sky?"

"It does, Earth. My kung fu teacher told me to let go, not to use physical strength, not to block the flow. Just let go. I didn't really get it. Until now, that is. I need to use the skills I have been shown on my journey to listen, to notice, to let go, until there is nothing. Then I will pass with ease."

Earth smiled at Sky." Then I'll let you be."

Sky crossed his legs, where he was sitting, and closed his eyes. For a moment it reminded him of the wise old man on the rock as a picture of him came into his head. He then let go of the image and focused his attention on his breath. Gently listening to the sound of his breath coming in and his breath coming out.

Thoughts invaded his mind, disturbing the quietness. He fidgeted briefly before refocusing on his breath. His mind quiet again, Sky noticed the sound of the gentle breeze as it blew over the tips of the grass. In the distance he could hear the sound of water, birds and creatures as they moved about.

Relaxed, his body became heavy, rooted to the spot like an immoveable rock. Letting go of what he was noticing, all feeling and sensations started to evaporate like the mist of the clouds, as the warmth of the sun shone through. All thoughts and feelings disappeared. He had entered a state of nothing.

Without thought, he stood up with his eyes closed and walked towards the edge of the mountaintop, where he had previously tried to jump across to the floating rock and peach tree. And instead of jumping across, he just continued to walk, right off the ledge. Instead of falling, as one might expect, his feet found a path, that earlier was not there. With ease he just walked straight across to the other side.

Standing next to the peach tree, he opened his eyes. He had done it. Walking around the peach tree, he noticed a plaque.

The Fruit of Eternal Youth

Still feeling peaceful from his meditation, he stood for a moment to take in the information. This was not what he had expected. He thought the peach would give him wisdom. That was the reason he had come on the journey. He looked over to Earth, who was now standing at the edge of a path she could not see, not daring to cross.

"The peach gives eternal youth, not wisdom as Tianlong told me," Sky said calmly.

"Is that what Tianlong said to you Sky, that the peach would give you wisdom?" Earth asked.

"No, he didn't," Sky said, realising the truth. "He said that I would find wisdom with the divine peach. And it's taken me until now to realise something important. And that is

155

that I have not found wisdom."

Earth looked confused.

"Wisdom can't be found," Sky continued. "Knowledge can be found or discovered, but wisdom can only be realised. And you've helped me realise this, Earth. It's like you helped wake something up inside me."

Earth was a little surprised by this. "That's very kind of you, Sky, but it was not me, it was you. All I shared with you is what I have learnt along the way."

"Yes, Earth, yes. You shared what you also learnt," Sky said in agreement. "And I'm grateful for that. It's not just me though, Earth, you have also realised a lot of things."

"You're right, Sky," Earth replied, recognising her own achievements. "I have realised not to judge so quickly. That includes myself as well as others. I've also realised that just because I'm scared of something, that doesn't mean I can't do it. Being scared is just a reminder for me to call on my courage, and do it anyway. I've learnt that I'm okay as I am, that we're okay, and we always were. We just needed to realise it. You know, it's kind of funny, Sky. We've come on this big journey - you to find wisdom and me to find my brother. In the end we have made good use of what we already knew. That's wisdom, Sky."

"Courage and Wisdom," Sky said with a smile. "Not a bad combination. Tianlong was right."

"So what about the peach, Sky? Are you going to eat the peach?" Earth asked.

"What, and gain eternal youth?" Sky asked, winking. "You know, it might just help us in finding your brother," Sky said, as he took a juicy peach from the tree. "How so?"

Earth asked. "Well, I think it will help me to always stay inquisitive, to search for and see the wonders around me, to have fun and see the best in things," Sky said.

"So, you'll help me find my brother then?" Earth replied.

"Absolutely," Sky said, before taking a bite of the peach. Wiping the juice from his mouth he added, "First though we must visit our parents, tell them what we have learnt. Tell them we are safe and that we have found each other."

"So, how do you feel?" Earth asked.

Sky's eyes brightened. "I feel, I feel FULLY ALIVE!" he roared.

With this, the wise old man, sitting on the rock, opened his eyes, smiled and said aloud, "And now the journey really begins," before closing his eyes again to meditate.

Coming soon...

The adventure continues...

The Guardian Lions

The Masters' Quest

Earth and Sky have completed their search for the Divine Peach. Now they must continue their journey to save Tao, before the warlord steals his power.

Frustrated by waiting for the right opportunity, Sky rushes to the gates of the warlord's village in an attempt to save Tao. But he is no match for the power of the warlord and is easily defeated.

Retreating back to his home, Sky hides in shame, refusing to join his friend Earth on her quest to save her brother. Desperate, Earth offers herself to the warlord in exchange for Tao. Now Sky must make a decision: deal with his shame and save his friend, or hide forever.

Offering help, Sky's father sends him to the Shaolin Temple to find the three masters. Each possesses a skill Sky will need to defeat the warlord and save Earth and Tao.

Coming soon...

The Guardian Lions

A World Beyond Our Own

A long time ago, when the minds of people were unmuffled by technology, many could see a world beyond our own. This was the world of dragons, unicorns and creatures. It was during this time, when these two worlds merged, that Earth and Sky lived to help save our world from destruction.

After the 'Great War on Creatures and Witches', the worlds once again parted. Only the lucky still had a window to this world. Through time, these windows closed one by one, until only a handful of lucky ones were left.

Now the windows to this world are being opened once again. If you are one of the lucky ones (which we all are), then this book is for you.

Get ready to learn about the world of the Guardian Lions and its creatures, the history and mystery, and how science is discovering what the ancient masters have known for thousands of years.

If you would like to be part of the adventures of Earth and Sky, you can get involved by visiting the website:

www.theguardianlions.co.uk

Free Newsletter...

Join the newsletter for insights into Earth and Sky's world, their training, the creatures, lion dance drumming and more...

Plus, by joining up for the free newsletter you will receive previews of their next adventures, and have the opportunity of becoming part of their story.

If you would like to train in the Shaolin arts, visit:
www.zenarts.co.uk or www.shaolin-training.com

Visit the website of the Grandmaster of my school at **www.shaolin.org**

If you would like the Guardian Lions to visit your school, be sure to pass this book onto ... you know who... in your school.

An insight into my inspirations

In 1977, my concept of reality was blown wide open by the Jedi Knights in Star Wars. I was 5 years old and anything was possible. In 1984 I was introduced to The Karate Kid, Daniel-san and Mr Miyagi and dreamt of meeting a master. Then in 1985 I was transported Back to the Future when a charming Marty McFly passed on an invaluable piece of advice to his would-be dad - If you put your mind to it you can accomplish anything.

I was deeply moved by these films and left with the thought...

Wow... if only I could develop the energy of the Jedis, be able to defend myself from bullies and accomplish anything I wanted!

After many years of study, applying my mind and making decisions, I not only became a master of Shaolin Kung Fu and Chi Kung, but also wrote this book. Proof that you can accomplish anything if you put your mind to it.

It is my pleasure and honour to share the wisdom of the masters with you.

Lightning Source UK Ltd.
Milton Keynes UK
UKOW02f0128250317
297499UK00002B/8/P